7.50

D1282157

# No-Fault Divorce

Michael Wheeler

# No-Fault Divorce

Beacon Press    Boston

Copyright© 1974 by Michael Wheeler

Beacon Press books are published under the auspices
of the Unitarian Universalist Association

Simultaneous publication in Canada by Saunders of Toronto, Ltd.

*All rights reserved*

Printed in the United States of America

9  8  7  6  5  4  3  2

Library of Congress Cataloging in Publication Data
Wheeler, Michael Allen, 1943-
    No-fault divorce.
    Bibliography: p. 187
    1. Divorce—United States.    I. Title.
KF535.W45        346'.73'0166        73-17421
ISBN 0-8070-4482-2

KF
535
.W45

# Contents

WITHDRAWN

145125   EMORY & HENRY LIBRARY

*For Candace*

# Acknowledgments

I spoke with scores of people while preparing this book — lawyers, judges, law professors, and, perhaps most important, people who have been or are in the process of being divorced. I am grateful to them all for sharing their experiences and insights with me. Almost everyone I interviewed generously allowed me to identify his statements. I have done so with one exception: I have used pseudonyms for those people whose experience with divorce is solely personal rather than professional. Some were willing to have their names known, but I see no reason for risking further unhappiness or embarrassment to them or their families. I have not, however, used any composite characters or cases.

Unfortunately I do not have space to thank here all who helped me, but I must acknowledge the assistance of some people whose interest went far beyond normal courtesy: Judges Grant L. Bowen, Walter Carpeneti, James Lawton, and Ralph Podell; Professors Homer Clark, Henry Foster, and Sanford Katz; attorneys Richard Dinkelspiel, Diana DuBroff, Regina Healy, George Lordan, Jr., Howard McKissick, Jr., Brooks Potter, Louise Raggio, Tim Savinar, and George Snyder; and also, Carol Delhaney Bangs, Nathaniel Denman, and Lewis Ohleyer. I am also grateful to the staffs of the libraries of Harvard Law School and New England School of Law — especially to Neil Cola at New England.

Had it not been for the encouragement and advice of David

Harrison, David Otte, Norman von Rosenvinge, and my father, Harry E. Wheeler, Jr., this book would not have been written. Finally, I am deeply obliged to Professor Richard Pearson of Boston University School of Law who read this manuscript at an earlier stage; all errors of fact or analysis are, of course, strictly my own.

M. W.

*Cambridge, Massachusetts*

# No-Fault Divorce

# Chapter One

# Anything but the Truth

Lester and Margaret Anderton were married in Cambridge, Massachusetts, in 1923. From the start they quarreled constantly. They separated several times, and whenever they got back together things seemed to be worse, not better. Lester moved out for good in 1931 but continued to send Margaret weekly checks for her living expenses. They had no children.

In 1973, after forty-two years of uninterrupted separation, Lester tried to get a divorce. He was an old man, incapacitated by a series of strokes, but he wanted to marry a woman he had met in his nursing home. Represented by a legal aid lawyer, he sued for divorce on the ground of "cruel and abusive treatment." Several years earlier, while he was recovering from his first stroke, Margaret had charged him with criminal nonsupport. When the judge dismissed her complaint, she rushed over to Lester, shouting insults and accusing him of faking his illness. Although most cruel and abusive divorce cases in Massachusetts involve physical blows, the lawyer believed that Lester's vulnerable condition made Margaret's behavior sufficiently cruel to constitute grounds.

Margaret contested the divorce, not out of any lingering affection for Lester, but because a divorce would terminate any right she might have to his Social Security payments, either as his wife or, as seemed imminent, his widow. Even though the Andertons had been separated for more than four decades, the trial judge denied the divorce, ruling that Margaret's misconduct was not an

1

adequate ground for divorce. Thus the Andertons remained married, if only in the eyes of the law.

The judge's decision illustrates the fault theory of divorce, a theory which prevails in most of the United States. To obtain a divorce it is not enough to show that your marriage is dead — as the Andertons' certainly was — you must establish that your spouse was was at fault for its death and you were free from blame. Moreover, the divorce statutes limit the grounds to several specified kinds of marital fault, typically cruelty, adultery, desertion, and drunkenness. The determination of what evidence is needed to prove grounds varies from state to state and court to court. It is possible, for example, that in states other than Massachusetts — or perhaps even before a different judge in Massachusetts — Lester Anderton would have been granted his divorce.

Even if the facts of a case seem clearly to constitute sufficient grounds, divorce may be denied if the legal pleadings are not technically correct. Ralph and Eva McNulty had been married twenty-three years, none of which had been happy. Both drank too much and often fought. Occasionally they had come to blows. Eva suspected her husband of being unfaithful, and once she had attempted suicide. The McNulty marriage, which had always been precarious, broke down completely after Ralph was convicted of committing incest with their thirteen-year-old daughter. His sentence, three to four years of hard labor, was not particularly severe, since he might also have been tried for statutory rape and criminal adultery. While Ralph was in prison, Eva sought a divorce in the Suffolk County (Massachusetts) Probate Court on the ground of cruel and abusive treatment. Ralph contested it because he was afraid that if it were granted, Eva would get sole title to their three-family house as a property settlement.

The trial judge denied Mrs. McNulty's petition for divorce. She appealed her case to Massachusetts' highest court. It upheld the denial, ruling that incest with the daughter was not cruel or abusive to the wife, in either a physical or emotional sense. Furthermore, the court declined to grant a divorce on basis of adultery — even though the facts clearly warranted it — because adultery had not been alleged as a ground, though it was implicit in the facts. Since Eva McNulty had not requested a divorce based specifically on adultery, the court would not volunteer to give her one. Its decision may seem Victorian, both in its through-the-looking-glass logic and its apparent distaste for divorce, yet it was handed down in 1956 and has not been overruled since then.

Do the Anderton and McNulty cases mean it is hard to get a divorce in Massachusetts and other fault states? That depends. For Lester Anderton and Eva McNulty the answer was clearly yes, but for thousands of other people the answer is no. Ten to thirty divorce cases are heard on an average day in the Suffolk County Probate Court and the great majority are granted. Most cases are brought by women who allege their husbands were cruel and abusive to them. Diane Currie is typical. She is thirty-seven and somewhat overweight. She is sitting in the back of the courtroom, her eyes fixed on the floor as she waits for her case to be called. Her younger sister Phyllis sits next to her; Phyllis is wearing a red suit and has had her hair done. Diane looks gray by comparison. Her lawyer is outside in the hall talking baseball with her husband's lawyer. Both have been through divorces many times before.

"Take the stand, Mrs. Currie." Diane Currie walks up to the witness stand, which in this courtroom is to the right of the judge, who according to rumor is stone deaf in his left ear. At first she looks straight ahead, but even though there are only fifteen people in a room which could seat two hundred, her glance soon sinks down.

"Please state your name and address to the court."

She answers so softly that the judge has to ask her to speak up. Even after she does, her answer does not carry beyond the first row of benches.

"Mrs. James Currie, 148 Hartney Street, Allston."

In a series of quick questions her lawyer asks to whom she is married (James Currie), how long she has lived at her present address (seven years), how many children she has (three), and when was the last time she and her husband lived together (October 18, 1973). He hands the clerk a marriage certificate.

"Now, Mrs. Currie, will you kindly tell the court what happened the evening of October 18, 1973?"

She draws a breath. "My husband came home in a bad mood. He had been drinking some. He swore at me and then slapped me in the face, hard. Then he walked out and he hasn't come back. After this happened, I called up my sister and she came right over."

Her husband's lawyer does not cross-examine Mrs. Currie and the judge says he does not want to hear any corroboration. Both lawyers approach the bench and hand the judge a separation agreement the Curries have already signed. It gives custody of the children to Mrs. Currie and provides her with thirty-five dollars a week alimony, plus fifteen dollars' support for each of the three children. The judge signs several papers which make the agreement part of his decree and Diane Currie has her divorce. It will be final in six months.

In the states which still subscribe to the fault theory, at least seventy-five percent of all divorces are based on cruelty. Roughly ninety percent are uncontested. Where financial matters and custody of children have been decided in advance, most cases can be disposed of in ten minutes or less. If you were to sit with your eyes closed in Room 233 of the Suffolk County Courthouse or in divorce courts in other parts of the country, you would think you were hearing Mrs. Currie's testimony over and over again: an angry husband; a cowering wife; sometimes a sister, mother, or friend who vouches for the story; divorce granted. The similarity of the proceedings is striking and, to many people, suspicious.

Most judges are reluctant to discuss perjury in divorce cases. Apparently they feel it is one thing for them to accept testimony which may be less than the whole truth, but another to admit doing so publicly. Judge Grant L. Bowen, who has heard eighteen thousand divorce cases while sitting on the Washoe County Court in Reno, is unusually candid about the practice in Nevada. To get a Reno divorce, you must state under oath not only that you have been in the state for six weeks, but also that you intend to stay there in the future. Most out-of-state people who appear in Reno for a divorce have a ticket in their pocket for a flight home that afternoon, yet they still swear that they plan to be Nevada residents. This kind of perjury does not bother Judge Bowen. "All that testimony about an 'indefinite stay' is just lawyer talk, a legal fiction. It doesn't make any sense for judges to try to fight the system." Many of his fellow judges in Massachusetts and other fault states who hear stories of cruelty like Mrs. Currie's probably feel the same way, even though few will say so openly.

In 1965 some New York judges did testify before a legislative committee that the existing law which restricted divorce to cases involving adultery was inducing flagrant perjury. A man who badly wanted a divorce would pay a private investigator to catch him in a hotel room with another woman in order to concoct acceptable evidence of adultery. Former Justice Meier Steinbrink stated that the "hotel evidence" cases invariably followed the same script. "She is always in a sheer pink robe. It's never blue — always pink. And he is always in his shorts when they catch them."

Lawyers are somewhat more willing to discuss perjury in divorce, but most say that they themselves do not permit their clients to lie. Brooks Potter, who has practiced family law in Boston for forty-five years, says, "I've never participated myself in a divorce where there is false testimony, but I am aware as you are that there are people who go into court and just plain fabricate blows and bad conduct on the part of the husband, or the wife as the case may be, in order to have grounds for divorce." Norman von Rosenvinge, who has practiced law almost as long, is more outspoken. "You know damn well that every judge who listens to that kind of story knows it's probably a lie. As long as people don't contradict themselves, most judges don't care."

Most people in the legal profession accept as axiomatic the notion that perjury is the rule in divorce courts, yet it is impossible to know its actual extent. When Mrs. Currie swore under oath that her husband struck her, she just may have been telling the truth. Certainly many couples who get divorced have fought, sometimes brutally, but because Diane Currie's story seems hackneyed, it evokes skepticism rather than sympathy.

Undoubtedly some cruelty cases are fabricated, but it is hard to measure the percentage — it may be ten percent or it may be ninety. The precise figure is moot, however, as appearance may be more important than reality: if lawyers and the general public believe that the fault system of divorce is corrupt, that in itself may justify changing it. Most legal scholars who have written about divorce have subscribed to such a belief. According to Monrad Paulsen, of the University of Virginia Law School, "The necessity of proving a ground of divorce such as adultery, cruelty, or desertion leads to the most flagrant collusion and outright fraud on the part of divorce-seeking couples."

Why is it that a court will deny a divorce for absurdly technical reasons one day, but willingly grant ten divorces on what may be perjured testimony the next? Part of the reason is historical. As it developed, Christianity taught that marriage was to be a permanent, lifelong relationship. In many cases, however, marriage provides emotional and physical trials which would test the will of saints. In England the ecclesiastical tribunals and parliament shared the power to dissolve marriages in special circumstances — social class counted more than personal need. In the United States, the courts were eventually given the sole power to grant divorce; this remedy was ostensibly limited to extraordinary situations where a person needed protection from the wrongdoing of his or her spouse. For the most part divorce was intended to preserve marriage by punishing those guilty of extreme marital misconduct, but the punishment — termination of the marriage — was often just what the wrongdoer sought. The divorce laws were never particularly effective. Robert Drinan, who taught family law at Boston College Law School before entering Congress, has stated that American divorce statutes were "impulsively enacted and carelessly drafted, on the supposition possibly that virtually no one really would make use of them. The implementation of the new laws was even worse."

From the outset one of the principal problems with divorce procedure has been its dependence on the adversary process. If a man is tried for murder, he will do his best to explain that he was nowhere near the scene of the crime, while the district attorney will produce witnesses who swear they saw the defendant pull the trigger. The judge and jury consider the conflicting testimony and arguments, and more often than not the truth — or something close enough to it — comes out. This adversary system works well in most areas of law, but only if there are two parties with opposing interests — a prosecutor and an accused criminal, a landlord and a tenant, or a driver and a pedestrian who was run down. If the conflict is real, both sides will dig up evidence and theories to support their case. The process thus generates enough information for the court to weigh in making its decision.

At least ninety percent of all divorces are uncontested, however; hence there usually is no dispute about the existence of grounds. In the great majority of divorces both the husband and the wife are willing to have the marriage end; one may want out more than the other, but the hesitant spouse often sees no sense in putting up a fight. Still the fault system requires one person — generally the wife — to sue the other in order to establish grounds, even though the decision to terminate the marriage was mutual. Because both people want the divorce, the husband does not contest it, so the court hears only the wife's story. Flimsy though it may be, if there is no testimony to contradict it, the evidence presented by the wife may be enough for the court to hang its hat on. Though the divorce itself may be uncontested, the husband may appear to be heard on questions of child custody or financial support, if the couple has not been able to work out an agreement on these points.

People usually allege only the barest of grounds where there is no real contest. If there actually are no facts which constitute grounds, cruelty is the easiest lie to tell. Even when there are other grounds, cruelty is usually alleged in order to spare everybody the embarrassment of a sordid story of adultery or the unhappy details of alcoholism. As a result the judge often knows nothing of what really caused the marriage to break up. One lawyer, David Levine, has observed, "The trial court is precluded from making its determination on the basis of the whole truth and must reluctantly honor the will of the parties like some official vending machine. The result is that the court's statement of facts, based as it is on minimal evidence, is often a restatement of the petitioner's version of the marital strife."

In theory a husband and wife are not permitted to agree to divorce, particularly if the grounds will be made up of facts which would provide a defense are to be withheld; but in practice this is done all the time. Although the court is often said to represent society's interest in preserving the marriage, it has little actual power to investigate the uncontradicted claims of the person seeking the divorce. Similarly, collusion is a defense which can be raised to prevent a divorce, but a person who has colluded with his or her spouse to end a marriage rarely will change his or her mind unilaterally. As a consequence judges may often suspect that grounds have been trumped up, but they have no means of knowing for sure.

The relative ease with which uncontested divorces are granted leads to an anomalous result. If the parties are still on good enough terms to work out an acceptable agreement on division of property and custody of children, they ordinarily will have no trouble getting a divorce on the basis of cruelty or some similar ground. But if the husband and wife have lost all respect for each other, if they want to use the courts to punish their spouse, if the divorce is contested, then there is a good chance the divorce will be denied. Eva McNulty's marriage, with the incest, the drinking, the fighting, and the attempted suicide, could not have been a more compelling case for divorce, but because of her failure to plead the right ground, the divorce was denied.

Some people believe the courts have no business deciding divorce. They feel that if a couple wants to divorce, or even if a person wants a divorce against the wishes of his or her spouse, the divorce should be granted automatically. The obstacle course established by the present divorce system obviously offends such people. Others contend that society has a valid interest in promoting family stability, pointing to statistics correlating broken homes with higher crime rates and increased welfare payments, as well as less tangible moral values. But even those who take a conservative view of family law should be dissatisfied with the fault system, and indeed many are. Discontent with fault-based divorce has become widespread, particularly in the past ten years. More than a dozen states have enacted major reforms of their divorce laws and almost all the rest are considering following their example. While there is heated debate about what shape reform ought to take, there is substantial agreement that fault divorce does not presently serve anyone's goals.

The most common criticism of the fault system is that it is hypocritical: it not only tolerates perjury, it encourages it. For many people, their first and most important experience with the legal system is divorce; currently there is one divorce granted in the United States for every three marriages performed. People's respect for the courts and the law must be diminished when they learn they cannot get a divorce if they tell the truth, but can if they lie about grounds or residency. That everyone else seems to be in on the sham — the lawyers and the judges — makes the whole system seem corrupt. The blatant hypocrisy has a personal cost as well. Ideally a divorce proceeding should deal with the realities of the marriage in a dignified way. It should clear the air, not cloud it. A divorce based on fictions and falsehoods demeans people who have usually suffered more than enough unhappiness.

Apparently there are many people who simply refuse to get a divorce if perjury is a prerequisite, but this does not mean that their marriages are preserved in any socially beneficial way. Sam Movalli served one hitch in Vietnam, then reenlisted for another while his wife and children stayed home. When he returned, he and his wife found, in his words, that they had "grown miles apart. We married sort of young, a lot happened to change us. Lorna talked to our lawyer and he said we didn't have grounds as it stood, but kind of implied that if Lorna said something about a fight and I went along with it, we could get a divorce. Neither of us wanted to get into any public name-calling, so we just haven't done anything about it." The Movallis have worked out a loose arrangement by which Sam sends Lorna a monthly check and he gets to see his son when on leave.

Lorna's description of the arrangement is not as sanguine as Sam's — he sometimes neglects to send a check — but she is willing to tolerate the situation at least for a while. "As far as we are concerned personally, we're already divorced. I guess if we ever want to remarry, we'll have to make it legal." In states with strict grounds, many people follow the Movallis' example. Similarly, if the desire to end the marriage is unilateral, the unhappy spouse always has the option of simply walking out. There are legal sanctions, both criminal and civil, against desertion, but many men and women prefer the small risk of a run-in with the law to sticking out a dead marriage. Strict laws can prevent the legal formality of a divorce, but they cannot force people to live together against their wills. That a state has a low divorce rate does not necessarily mean it has a high level of family stability. People can and do dissolve their marriages emotionally, socially, and economically without the help of the courts. Sometimes they remarry, thereby committing the crime of bigamy, and have children who are illegitimate in the eyes of the law. Concern about these so-called "irregular unions" has been one of the arguments for reform.

Getting divorced in your home state can be expensive. The

adversary process, the difficult collateral issues involving property and children, and the technical complexities of the laws all make the process of divorcing far more complicated, hence more costly, than the process of marrying. Lawyers' fees vary widely, but often they are high enough to be a real burden on a middle-class family. For people who are less well off economically, the cost of divorce may be prohibitive, if legal aid is not available. Henry Foster, who teaches at New York University School of Law, has concluded, "Poverty usually promotes extralegal action rather than a resignation to and endurance of an intolerable situation. The poor resort to desertion and propagate illegitimate children in large numbers because law has priced itself out of the market."

The present divorce system is often criticized for being inconsistent: cases with identical facts can come to opposite results. Misconduct that constitutes cruelty in Nevada may be insufficient in Massachusetts. Each state has sovereignty over marriages and divorces within its jurisdiction; it can make both as restrictive or as lenient as it pleases, and, within certain broad bounds, its policy will be respected by its sister states. Congress does not have power to enact a national divorce law, and it's doubtful that all the states will voluntarily adopt identical standards and procedures.

As a result, "migratory divorce" has been a big business. Over the years tens of millions of dollars have been spent in Nevada by citizens of other states looking for easy divorce. At different times Alabama, Arkansas, and a few other states have had the reputation of being divorce mills. Lorna Movalli considered going to Reno, but discovered she could not afford it. "My lawyer here wanted three hundred dollars for setting it up and the lawyer out there was going to get three-fifty. Even if I just stayed in a boarding house, it was going to cost a lot by the time six weeks were over. Counting air fare, I figured it was going to cost fifteen hundred dollars at a bare minimum and we just don't have that kind of money to spend." Most people cannot afford the time or money that migratory divorce requires; thus it has been an escape open only to relatively prosperous people.

Even within the boundaries of one state, the divorce laws can be inconsistently applied. As the contrast between the Anderton and Currie cases illustrates, the existence of a contest is more important in determining whether there will be a divorce than the actual condition of the marriage. Most uncontested cases are granted as a matter of course, but there are sometimes exceptions. Shortly before Florida did away with fault divorce, a chancellor in one case ruled, "I don't think he [the husband] has shown any grounds that I am willing to accept at all, but I am going to divorce them. They both want it, don't they?" The chancellor's decision was reversed by a higher court; had he only said he had found grounds, his decision probably would have stood. In the future he may be more tactful and less honest in his written opinions.

Because the divorce laws grant judges a great deal of discretion in deciding cases, the outcome can depend on who happens to hear the case. Several years ago the Michigan Law Revision Commission reported, "The most frequently used ground in Michigan and most other states is extreme cruelty, a vague term which can be applied loosely by liberal judges and strictly by those who believe in the indissolubility of marriage." The personal biases of judges show through in divorce perhaps more frequently than in other areas of law. One Massachusetts judge has the reputation among local lawyers of "going haywire" if he learns that a woman seeking divorce is receiving welfare assistance.

Judges view their responsibilities differently. Some, feeling divorce is a private matter, particularly if it is uncontested, are reluctant to interfere; but there are others who believe they have a constant duty to uphold the interests of the state regardless of the wishes of the husband and wife. Judge James Lawton of Massachusetts is in the latter category. "Take the average family. They have a tough time making ends meet. If the husband leaves the home, he's going to have to pay additional rent for a room or an apartment and maybe payments on another car. He's going to spend a lot more on food. All this adds up fast. When a divorce is before me, the people are already separated, but they're both trying to make a good impression by being as thrifty as possible. Once I grant the divorce, the husband is going to start missing some of the support payments or the wife is going to have trouble with expenses. It's a fact of life. There just isn't enough money to go around. So before you know it, the family is on welfare.

Maybe I can't always stop that from happening, but I'll do everything I can to delay it." Some judges try to stall the divorce proceedings in hopes of a reconciliation, while others feel it is wise to get matters settled quickly and cleanly, so people can adjust to their new roles.

The moral outlook of the presiding judge also affects the character of the hearing. One Boston lawyer observes that, "The oppressiveness varies from court to court. If you go to one county you find that the woman must stand twenty feet from the judge. Her lawyer has to scream his questions to her and she has to scream her answers to the judge. In the neighboring county, the lawyer whispers to his client and she whispers to the judge."

The fault system is inconsistent, expensive, and hypocritical. As serious as these shortcomings are, the system might be tolerable if it somehow contributed to family stability in our society. But it does not. If anything it obscures the real issues in marital breakdown, and thus makes their solution all the more difficult. The fundamental weakness of fault divorce is that it is predicated on the myth that the breakdown of a marriage can be attributed solely to the wrongdoing of one spouse.

The premise is wrong on two counts. First a fight, whether it is a petty squabble or an out-and-out brawl, is seldom the fault of just one person. When we mediate a fight between two children, two adults, or, for that matter, two nations, the threshold question is always "Who started it?" but it is a question which rarely gets a satisfactory answer. A husband may punch his wife but claim he was provoked. A wife may desert her husband but say she has good reason to leave. A person's motivation for committing adultery may be even deeper than he or she understands. Second, wrongdoing is not the only thing that can kill marriages. Time changes people, people can grow apart, and marriage can die a natural death. These observations are so familiar they risk being trite; yet fault divorce is blind to the realities of marriage. At its occasional best it deals only with manifestations of marital breakdown, but it never goes to its roots.

Pigeonholing cases into a few specified grounds leads the judge, the lawyers, and, most importantly, the parties to deal with the symptoms rather than the underlying causes of marital problems. The fault system is oversimplified and often inflexible. Sometimes it prevents divorce when a marriage is clearly dead, as in the Anderton case; but it can also condone divorce where it might be hasty. Kinsey and his successors have reported that adultery is a widespread phenomenon in our society; many marriages are able to survive it and some apparently thrive on it. Yet the fault system gives a person whose spouse has committed adultery an automatic ticket for divorce. It makes no difference whether the spouse was deeply involved in a long affair or had a single foolish fling. One act of adultery is enough. If the innocent spouse wants a divorce, it must be granted, no matter what the judge or anyone else thinks about the long-term chances for saving the marriage.

The rigidity of the fault system forces people to characterize their cases, with the guidance of lawyers, in such a way that they fit the grounds. Incompatibility, whether of temperament, goals, or values, is probably the basic cause of many divorces; but it is not recognized as a ground in the written law of the fault states. Yet according to sociologist Jessie Bernard, it is widely allowed in practice "either by collusion or by way of some other legal dodge of one kind or another. Cruelty is probably the commonest cover for incompatibility." That the laws are not always applied as strictly as they are written alleviates some of the hardship of fault-based divorce, yet as will be explained in subsequent chapters, many of the unfortunate vestiges remain.

The emphasis on establishing grounds makes people whose marriages are in trouble ask, "*Can I* get a divorce?" rather than "*Should we* get a divorce?" The requirement of proving fault makes divorce seem like an individual problem instead of a mutual one. Sometimes it is the wedge which drives apart a couple who might otherwise have been able to work out their difficulties. Anthropologist Paul Bohannan states, "Both marriage counselors and lawyers have assured me that reconciliation is always more difficult after grounds have been discussed and legal papers written than when it is still in the language of 'reasons' and personal emotion. Legal language and choice of grounds are the first positive steps toward a new type of relationship with the person one of my informants called 'my ex-to-be.' "

The adversary nature of fault divorce can add to a me-against-you momentum which is hard to stop. A husband, who has been threatened with divorce, sees his lawyer, who warns him to withdraw all his money from their joint accounts. He does so, hiding it in safe deposit boxes or trusts, just in case his wife really means it. When she finds out that the bank accounts are empty, she will understandably retaliate and the marital harassment will escalate. According to Texas attorney Lee Hawke, "Some marriages will end because the parties got caught up in the judicial process and do not know how to get out." Even if there is a waiting period between the time the divorce is instituted and the hearing is held, "The big step having already been taken by filing for divorce, the client may be too embarrassed to speak up and stop all the legal machinery that has been put in motion."

Requiring one person to find fault with the other aggravates an already unhappy situation and further diminishes whatever chance there might be of salvaging the marriage. Even if the divorce is sought on the relatively mild ground of cruelty, one spouse may be tempted to feel vindicated, while the other may resent being unfairly accused. Resentments multiply and their effects are often felt by the children. Two law professors, Joseph Goldstein and Max Gitter, have concluded that "Perhaps the most damaging result of a 'fault'-based divorce procedure is that it exacerbates the aggressive forces that may be already undermining the family. It dissipates family emotional and financial resources at a time when they are most needed. The hatred, bitterness, and resentment fed by a drawn-out divorce are likely to destroy the possibility of conciliation and distort the negotiations and proceedings designed to resolve the very difficult and emotionally freighted issues of finances and child custody."

Even where divorce is clearly appropriate, where there is no chance or sense in reconciliation, the fault system causes harm. A divorce ends the marriage, but it does not terminate all the relationships between the husband and wife. In most instances the husband is required to pay support to his former spouse, and, if she has custody of their children, he will likely have some rights of visitation. Some studies have shown that at least one out of every three divorces involving minor children is followed by still more litigation. When the proportion of cases with serious problems not brought to the court is also considered, it seems likely there is deep dissatisfaction after most divorces. By ending marriages on a bitter note, the fault system discourages people from adjusting responsibly to their new roles.

Another weakness of the fault system is that only the "innocent" spouse can ask for a divorce. A man who has committed adultery cannot use his act as grounds. In such a case, the wife has the sole power to decide whether there will be a divorce. Some women might want one, but in certain circumstances many others would be hesitant. A delay would help some couples sort out their problems, but if a husband is persistent in his desire to end the marriage, his wife's refusal to seek the divorce will probably make things worse for everybody involved. He will retaliate in hopes of proving to her the marriage is not worth saving. She may relent, but she may also be tempted to get back at him with her most powerful weapon, her veto on the divorce. He can bellow, stomp, and slug, but she can deny him what he wants most. Unless she has acted in a way which would give him grounds, he is stuck; even if she has, she may still be able to prevent divorce by raising the defense of recrimination, described later.

This can ultimately lead to a situation in which the husband (or the wife if the roles are reversed) has to buy his or her way out of the marriage. If it is the husband who must purchase his wife's consent, he will have to pay far more in alimony and child support. If it is the wife who wants out, she may have to agree to give up any financial help from her husband; she may even have to forfeit custody of her children. The final arrangement does not reflect the needs and resources of the parties but how desperately one person wanted to get out and how hard a bargain the other was able to drive. It may prove to be a Pyrrhic victory for the spouse who extorts a big settlement. The terms may be so unreasonable and resentments which were created during the negotiation may be so deep that it will never be carried out.

That a divorce is not contested in court does not necessarily mean it was not bitterly fought beforehand. The requirement of proving fault puts the parties in an uneven bargaining position and settlements which are worked out are often unfair. If a couple has signed a separation agreement, the court will take only a cursory look at it. There are instances, of course, where a couple cannot agree to divorce; if the spouse who wants out cannot establish grounds, then there will be no divorce. In all likelihood the marriage will continue in name only, a relationship described by some lawyers as "holy deadlock" of the "bonds of acrimony."

The various defenses a person can invoke to prevent divorce even where fault has been proven have bizarre and unfortunate effects. Condonation is the most frequently raised defense. If a man discovers that his wife has committed adultery but continues to live with her, he may be barred from using her adultery as a ground for divorce. Condonation reflects the notion that the "innocent" husband in this case should not be able to have it both ways: either his wife's adultery so offended him that it broke up their marriage or it did not. He should not be allowed to continue to live with her while holding the threat of divorce over her head.

The doctrine of condonation may have some theoretical appeal, but it makes little sense in practice. If the husband sees his lawyer about his wife's infidelity, the first thing he will be told is that if he does not leave home, he may lose his right to have a divorce. Arthur Fox, a Virginia attorney, has noted that the "practical effect of the rule of condonation is to impose a 'do-or-die' decision upon the innocent spouse in the hour of crisis. Confronted suddenly with the knowledge of his partner's infidelity, he must decide promptly whether to pack his suitcase and leave what may have been and could be a very happy home, or to continue marital relations thereby forfeiting the right to dissolve the marriage if it should subsequently cease to be viable." The doctrine of condonation does not allow the couple the unrestricted opportunity to try to work things out. If the husband and wife are separated, their chances of reconciling are bound to be much less than if they are still living together. On the other hand, if they do live together, even the best-intended efforts may not succeed. Some states have abolished the defense of condonation and others have modified it, but it still applies in half the states. Where it persists, it tends to undermine family stability by blocking off the best avenue to reconciliation.

The doctrine of recrimination, the other important defense, provides that if both parties are at fault, there can be no divorce. The law refuses to dirty its hands if it considers both the husband and wife wrongdoers. Usually a couple will conceal from the court the fact that both parties have grounds; technically this constitutes collusion or fraud on the court. Nevertheless, the recrimination defense is sometimes used. George Lordan, Jr., a Cambridge lawyer, represented a woman who was sued by her husband for a divorce based on cruel and abusive treatment. She had nagged him, cut his clothing into little pieces, and thrown china at him. Lordan says, "It was a terrible marriage. They both went out with other people and fought a lot. But she was full of spite and just didn't want to let her husband have the satisfaction of divorcing her. I explained that because he wasn't giving her much money anyway, a divorce wasn't going to hurt her financially, and I tried to convince her not to fight it, but she insisted. As an attorney, I'm paid to do what a client wants — I can't play God with people — so I introduced evidence of his adultery. That was recrimination and the judge denied the divorce. They're separated and they're never going to get back together. It's ridiculous."

The recrimination doctrine forces unhappily married couples to remain married, if only in a legal sense. As a result, it encourages adulterous affairs, illegitimacy, and desertion, while preventing the stability which might come with remarriage. The legislatures of a number of states, having recognized that attempts to punish mutual marital misconduct by a life sentence to an unhappy marriage actually undercuts family well-being, have abolished the defense of recrimination. It is still valid, however, in many jurisdictions.

The concept of fault not only is unrealistic in terms of the real causes of marital breakdown, but it also fails to provide guidance for the solution of the financial and custody problems which often arise. Fault encourages people to look to the courts for personal vindication. Victory is measured in dollars, whether by the husband who "won't give her a dime" or the wife who wants to "take him for everything he's got." In most states alimony awards are often punitive, though they are not generally supposed to be. The more at fault the husband seems, the more he pays. If it is the wife who is allegedly at fault for ruining the marriage, then she receives less. People use evidence of fault to try to prove that their spouse is unfit to care for the children, who become hostages in matrimonial warfare.

The shortcomings of fault-based divorce are not new, but it is only recently that people have become concerned about the magnitude. For those who believe the right to divorce should be as free as an individual's right to marry, any kind of state regulation is repugnant. But even those who feel society has an important interest in protecting family stability are coming to see that fault divorce fails in this very respect. Representative Drinan, whose attitudes about marriage are more conservative than most of his politics, has concluded, "The judicial process for obtaining divorce in America — employing grounds and defenses — was never and is not now a sensible or suitable legal method for a case involving divorce."

Most people agree the time has come to change our divorce laws, but there is no consensus about what kind of change there ought to be.

# Chapter Two

# Divorce Reform in California

In California it is impossible to get a divorce.

The California legislature abolished divorce as of 1970, replacing it with what is called "dissolution of marriage." The legislature did far more than create a new name for termination of marriage. It also eliminated all the fault-related grounds, such as adultery and extreme cruelty, and in their place substituted a no-fault standard, "irreconcilable differences, which have caused the irremediable breakdown of the marriage." There is a second ground, "incurable insanity," but it was used in only a handful of cases in the past, so for all practical purposes "irreconcilable differences" is now the sole basis for dissolution of marriage in California.

The new law grew out of sweeping proposals which had been made by the Governor's Commission on the Family, a bipartisan group of lawyers, judges, law professors, politicians, and other professionals appointed by Governor Edmund Brown in 1965 to draft revisions in California's family laws. In addition to the abolition of fault divorce, the commission had proposed new standards for determination of custody and support, establishment of special family courts and mandatory pre-trial counseling for those seeking to dissolve their marriages. Many of these recommendations were controversial; for political reasons discussed in Chapter Eight, the legislature ultimately rejected some suggestions and modified others.

The commission had built a strong case against fault divorce, and its argument against it was widely accepted, at least in principle, by both politicians and the public. The commission's proposal had stated that "in addition to simplifying the procedures and permitting the proper full inquiry by the court, the removal of the specific fault ground and the adoption of a 'breakdown of marriage' standard will eliminate much of the adversary aspect of divorce litigation by removing the need for specific accusation and answer. It will prevent the use of misconduct not formally alleged as a bludgeon (by threat of its disclosure) in obtaining extortion concessions concerning support and the division of property from the opposing spouse — concessions which are frequently inequitable and unworkable, and which do not represent any true agreement. Moreover, it will put an end to the dissimulation, hypocrisy — and even outright perjury — which is engendered by the present system. . . ." It is doubtful that many people thought no-fault would be a panacea, but the feeling against the old California law ran surprisingly deep considering that it had been interpreted very liberally.

The new law does away with most of the adversary trappings which accompany divorce. To lessen hostilities, all pleadings are stated in a neutral form, so instead of being called "Mary Smith versus John Smith," a case is now listed as "In re the marriage of John and Mary Smith." It is no longer necessary to point the finger of fault at one spouse or the other, so either can start a proceeding to dissolve the marriage. Thus a man or woman who is having an affair can initiate a divorce, while under traditional notions of law, he or she would be considered "at fault," and thus be barred from doing so.

Most significantly, the standard for judicially terminating marriage was changed. As Edward Raskin, chairman of the Family Law Committee of the California Bar Association when the law went into effect, put it, "If a woman says she can't stand living with a man because he snores, that is an irreconcilable difference regardless of the fact he can't help himself. Previously, snoring would not have been considered cruelty. But if a woman just can't stand living with a man, or vice versa, that would be enough."

The wording of the no-fault standard was not quite the same

as the commission had proposed. The phrases "irreconcilable differences" and "irremediable breakdown" were the products of hasty compromise, notwithstanding the long and careful work which preceded legislative debate. For example, the redundancy of keeping "incurable insanity" as a second ground indicates that the final version of the bill was not fully thought through — it is impossible to imagine a judge who could deny there was an irremediable breakdown of the marriage in the face of incurable insanity.

Far more perplexing is the meaning of irreconcilable differences and irremediable breakdown. If taken at face value, these phrases present a standard so strict that no marriage could ever be dissolved, for who is to say there is absolutely no chance for any marriage to survive, read literally, the statute might seem to preclude dissolution even if the chances of reconciliation were only one in a million. Obviously no one intended to apply the new test so stringently; still it should be understood that there is nothing inherent in the marriage-breakdown theory which necessarily makes it "easier" — in the familiar sense of that word — than traditional divorce law.

Other sections of the statute may have been intended to clarify the new standard, but if anything they made it more obscure: "Irreconcilable differences are those grounds which are determined by the court to be substantial reasons for not continuing the marriage and which make it appear that the marriage should be dissolved." Herma Kay, a law professor at Berkeley who was a moving force on the commission, was particularly disturbed by the references to "grounds" in this definition because "it calls to mind traditional notions of fault and thus may lead some attorneys and judges to approach the new law as though 'irreconcilable differences' were merely a new name for 'mental cruelty.'" This danger was partially mitigated by still another portion of the law which prohibits, to an extent, the introduction of evidence of specific acts of marital misconduct. Justice Mosk of the California Supreme Court has stated that he thinks the new standard for divorce was supposed to be unclear, adding, "Seldom have code provisions given trial courts less definitive direction; this tolerance, I suggest, was deliberate and is desirable in a field as volatile as proceedings for termination of the marital status."

Whether or not the ambiguity of the new law was intentional, its wording has been criticized from many quarters. Nevertheless, there has been relatively little disagreement in the courtroom about what the new no-fault standard is supposed to be. Most lawyers and judges believe that irreconcilable differences are proven to exist if the married couple — or even just one spouse — says they do. Under the commission's proposal a judge would have been compelled to grant dissolution if one person persisted in asking for it, regardless of the wishes of his or her spouse; but, according to the wording of the final version of the law, judges seem to have discretion to deny dissolution. However, in almost every case, the act of going into court and requesting dissolution is taken as conclusive evidence that the marriage has broken down and judges usually make no further inquiry. Lewis Ohleyer, the Domestic Relations Commissioner in San Francisco, observes that "under the new system, there is no need for witnesses; there is no need to testify about the underlying reasons for the break-up. Some of the more conservative judges, particularly Catholics, asked more questions at first, but the legislative intent made clear this was not to be their function." As the new law has been applied, if one person says the marriage has broken down and the other says it has not, that in itself may be considered an irreconcilable difference.

If people have agreed in advance on a property settlement and custody of the children, appearance in court is a formality. Recognizing this, the Contra Costa County Court established a procedure which allowed some cases to be handled entirely by affidavits mailed to the court; neither spouse was required to appear in court personally. The national media played up the practice, calling it "mail order divorce," and compared it to other California cultural innovations like drive-in church. According to Ohleyer, "The press coverage was unfair to what they were really doing there. It was discretionary with the judge. If he knew both lawyers and respected their integrity, he might not see any purpose in having people come in just to see if they had signed the various papers. But many affidavits were turned down, either because the judge did not know the lawyers, or because he wanted to learn more about the family situation." In 1972 California's Supreme Court, in *In re the Marriage of McKim,* ruled that unless there are exceptional circumstances, such as hospitalization or imprisonment, the person seeking dissolution must appear in court, so there is no longer divorce by mail. Nevertheless, most dissolution hearings are hardly trials in either a legal or emotional sense.

Tim Savinar, a partner in a small San Francisco law firm, enjoys what he calls the "counseling and negotiating aspects" of his domestic practice but thinks the hearings are tedious and pointless. "Beforehand I just tell my client I'm going to ask five questions — they're all leading questions — and that they should answer 'yes' to all of them. It's a little ritual:

*Lawyer:* Have you been a resident of California for six months and of the county for two months before the filing of petition?
*Client:* Yes.
*Lawyer:* Is it true there are no children?
*Client:* Yes.
*Lawyer:* Is this your signature on the marital agreement?
*Client:* Yes.
*Lawyer:* And does this represent a complete accounting of all the property that you wished to have settled by the court and all your rights for spousal support?
*Client:* Yes.
*Lawyer:* Is it true there have arisen in your marriage irreconcilable differences which you and your husband have attempted to remedy, but which you have been unable to overcome?
*Client:* Yes.

And that's all it takes. The light goes off, the bell rings — divorce granted."

Savinar thinks that there is no reason for wasting the court's time — and his — in such matters. "After I finish, I say, 'Does your honor have any questions?' He asks one or two of the exact same questions I just asked. It always happens because the judge is not paying any attention at all. And that really points out the folly of requiring a hearing. Where there is a marital settlement and the other guy has defaulted, you can program all the relevant questions ahead of time. The judge asks a few things just to show he is awake, and it usually proves that he's asleep."

To a great extent, then, no-fault divorce in California has become no-grounds divorce. If one person wants to end the marriage, he or she can do it merely by request. According to Herma Kay, that divorce is now available on demand is not very different from the old practice. "It's just under a new rubric. The mental cruelty divorces were divorce on demand as far as I can tell. I don't remember many contested cases being denied, once the courts determined ways to grant a wife support."

Although the end result may be much the same, the new law has simplified the process of getting a divorce. For the most part, people's reactions to the changes have been positive. One man who had been married eight years described it as "all very painless and civilized." Perhaps not surprisingly, his former wife took the opposite view, saying it was "too impersonal and cold-blooded. I wanted a chance to tell the judge how hard I tried to make our marriage succeed, and the anguish I went through before filing for divorce." Judge Byron Lindsley believes that her reaction is not uncommon. Some women seem disappointed in the no-fault hearing, because they "want their husbands to permanently bear the brand of guilt." If some people miss the melodramatics of divorce, the judges themselves are happy to be spared it. Judge William Jale hears as many as twenty cases a day and appreciates the difference that no-fault has made. "Instead of screaming and name-calling, we have a business proposition that goes off fairly simply." One young woman was pleased that the hearing was quick and simple — "I was surprised when the judge said, 'That will be all.'" — but like many others she would have preferred not having to appear in court at all.

Under the new law, most cases are routine, taking only a few minutes of the court's time, but where there are bitter disputes over custody or financial matters, the atmosphere can be as hostile as it ever was under the old fault system. One lawyer states that "changing the law and procedures has quieted things down in most cases, but if people really want to cut each other's throats, they're going to do it." He says that he will take a simple divorce for several hundred dollars, but if he senses a real contest over the collateral issues, he will demand two thousand dollars in advance.

Ostensibly the new law prohibits evidence of marital fault from being introduced in court, except in custody disputes, but attorneys have found ways of getting it before the judge in hopes of swaying his decision on spousal support. Kathryn Gehrels, a San Francisco attorney, says that "some lawyers drag in fault by making a custody issue in every case and others get it in indirectly by asking questions like, 'Didn't you take a trip to Hawaii with Miss So-and-so for whom you paid all the costs?' " That marital fault is no longer the test for divorce has not meant that each and every divorce is neat and painless, but it does seem to have reduced the emotional trauma for many couples.

The substance of the law — the notion that divorce can apparently be had for the asking without resorting to accusations — has been accepted by the general public and most of the bar, but there are some lawyers who have misgivings. Harry Fain, a Beverly Hills attorney, publicly expressed his concern during the 1972 American Bar Association convention at which no-fault divorce was vigorously debated. "The Governor's Commission did not want to reach the point where, in effect, we give divorce on demand, because we know marriage is an institution that is being seriously threatened. But our present court proceedings are only one- or two-minute affairs with just a few questions asked. The parties don't even end their marriage with a decent respectable burial. What concerns us is that if we erode further the commitment to marriage with the idea you can get out of it so easily, we are not doing a service to society."

Fain does not want a return to the fault system, but regrets that the legislature enacted only part of the commission's proposals. "We originally recommended some kind of mandatory inquiry in which somebody would look into the status of the marriage, the children, and the family, so we just don't rubber stamp marriages out of existence. This was totally misconstrued or distorted in the legislative debate. Opponents said there weren't enough marriage counselors to do all this work, but we hadn't envisioned taking dead marriages and trying to counsel them back into existence. We just wanted to keep the door open for people who wanted help or who wanted to consider keeping their marriage alive."

It is unlikely the legislature will direct judges to scrutinize cases more carefully, but the California Supreme Court's opinion in McKim, requiring a personal appearance in court, might be read by some as authorizing judges to do more than rubber stamp every petition for dissolution. In McKim the majority of the court contended that the legislature had rejected the commission's proposal that one person be able to terminate a marriage unilaterally, regardless of the wishes of his or her spouse. From this it concluded that "Although the Legislature intended that as far as possible dissolution proceedings be nonadversary, eliminating acrimony, it did not intend that findings of the existence of irreconcilable differences be made perfunctorily." The court then ruled that the trial judge, "not the parties, must decide whether the evidence adduced supports findings that irreconcilable differences do exist and that the marriage has broken down irremediably and should be dissolved."

Lower court judges are reluctant to criticize the opinions of their state supreme court, in part as a matter of propriety and also out of recognition that the higher court will in time review many of their own decisions. Nevertheless, some judges privately feel McKim is a flagrant misreading of the purpose of the new law. One, who asked not to be identified, said, "The Assembly committee specifically filed a legislative history, which is not usually done, and in it they said that if one party wants a dissolution, the court cannot interfere. It must grant the dissolution. So the legislative intent is different from what the Supreme Court ruled, but I've taken an oath to uphold the law as they interpret it, so I have to go along with it."

Another judge, Walter Carpeneti of San Francisco, believes McKim will change the dissolution proceedings, though probably not radically. "Before the decision, most judges felt that if one party wanted dissolution, it was automatic and all he or she had to say was that there were irreconcilable differences which led to an irremediable breakdown, but now the Supreme Court seems to indicate that there should be something more than that." Judge Carpeneti does not think McKim requires a return to the old adversary system, "but it would admit in part the specific acts of cruelty which had supposedly been made inadmissible except in question of custody. I've taken the case to mean that if the parties have been separated for six months or a year and have drawn up a settlement agreement and there are no minor children, then that alone is sufficient. I'm not bound, of course, but why would they go to all that trouble unless in their mind — not in some psychiatrist's or marriage counselor's mind, but in their mind — irreconcilable differences have really arisen. And that's the key." He does not expect *McKim* to restrict dissolution of marriage, though he thinks it does give judges authority to make a deeper inquiry where there are young children or where the decision to end the marriage seems hasty.

Lawrence Stottert, the chairman of the California Bar Association's Family Law Committee, does not think *McKim* has had much impact other than requiring the petitioning party to show up in court. "The courts have indicated that they want to see somebody's face and ask a few questions. Personally, I feel that the need for this is minimal, but actually most people want to go to court and anybody who is interested in getting a divorce can afford the five minutes it takes to appear." Stottert sees no problem in dispensing with court appearances and handling the whole procedure through notarized affidavits. "The amount of fraud that is being committed on the court is negligible. And anyone who wants to lie can do it under oath on the stand just as well as by affidavit."

At this point it is hard to predict the long-run impact of the *McKim* decision. At the moment its influence seems limited to the procedural aspects of divorce, rather than the substantive standard. It has curtailed divorce by affidavit, but, though some judges appear to be going through the motions of making a more careful inquiry into the existence of irreconcilable differences, there do not seem to be any petitions for dissolution being denied.

The precise interpretation of the statute may be somewhat in flux, but the practical effect of no-fault divorce in California has already been dramatically clear. In 1970, the first year under the new law, the number of dissolutions jumped forty-six percent. The figure dipped slightly in 1971, but headed back up in 1972. The increase is ironic because when Governor Brown appointed his commission in 1965 he directed it to begin a "concerted assault on the high incidence of divorce in our society and its often tragic consequences." He added, "Whatever the cause of our growing divorce rate — the anxieties in our world, a society of rootlessness and increasing mobility, an erosion of the moral absolute — divorce produces not only broken homes but broken lives. It erodes the very foundation of our society, the family." At first it was expected that the commission would recommend tightening up the laws to make divorce much harder to obtain; as a result, some people rushed to the courts to end their marriages before any new law went into effect.

It would be misleading to say that no-fault increased the rate of divorce in California by forty-six percent, as there are a number of factors behind the absolute increase. A growing population was bound to push the number of divorces up somewhat, particularly now that the "baby boom" generation has reached the age of marriage and divorce. Other changes in the law, such as the guidelines for division of property and custody of children, may have broken stalemates where a couple could not agree on the price of a divorce. Expanded legal assistance to low-income families through government-funded or law-school—affiliated programs has made the legal system accessible to many people who could not afford the cost of retaining a private lawyer for divorce.

Nevertheless, most of the increase in dissolutions can be traced in one way or another to the removal of proving fault. Lewis Ohleyer states, "Under the old system some people were willing to go into court and swear to things that weren't true, if that's what it took to get a divorce, but there were other people who wouldn't compromise themselves. And then others just didn't want to drag their personal problems into court." Judge Carpeneti agrees. "The fact people had to come into court and wash their dirty linen in public kept some from going ahead with divorce. The simpler and cleaner you make the process, the more people are going to use it."

The increase reflects not just how many people are now getting divorced, but where they are doing it. At the same time divorces in California shot up, the number in Nevada went down. In 1970 it dropped roughly fifteen percent. California has not become a competitor for the national divorce business — it requires six months residency, as opposed to Nevada's six weeks — but Californians who previously went out of state to end their marriages now find it easier to stay home. State Senator Donald Grunsky, who was one of the sponsors of no-fault divorce, is pleased with this consequence of the new law. "Californians are now settling their domestic differences in our courts instead of going out of state, and that is all to the good."

In 1970 twenty percent of all divorces in the United States were granted in California. Although reform there was initially intended to decrease the number of divorces, few people seem disturbed that the law has had an opposite effect. Richard Dinkelspiel, a San Francisco lawyer who was cochairman of the commission, says, "I think the increase is a good sign. Until we had this law, a lot of people separated, lived with other people, and had children whose legal status was cloudy. It's healthy that people are getting legal, orderly dissolutions."

Although no-fault divorce has existed in California for only a few years, the experience there offers some lessons to other states considering adopting it. First, the most carefully conceived and drafted proposal can be chewed to shreds in the legislative process. Compromises made hurriedly during heated debate often prove to be worse than the two competing alternatives — half a loaf is not always better than none. The political background of the California law is discussed in greater depth in Chapter Eight. Second, though some people contend that any divorce statute should be ambiguous, so as to give the trial judge latitude in deciding cases, ambiguity could conceivably lead to uneven justice. Max Rheinstein, an eminent legal scholar, thinks that the problem of interpreting "irremediable breakdown of the marriage" is less than meets the eye. "True enough, this term is susceptible of a great variety of interpretations, especially when, as the statute says, the breakdown must be caused by irreconcilable differences. A conservative judge may use this formula to deny the dissolution of a marriage in situations in which under the former law a divorce might have been had for the asking, upon true or faked evidence. But are California trial judges likely to be conservative? Few have been so in the past."

Herma Kay is less willing to dismiss the problem of ambiguity. As a member of the Governor's Commission she had supported making divorce mandatory if one person wanted it as a "guard against the objection that the breakdown principal allows a judge who dislikes divorce to require the perpetuation of hopeless marriages under the guise of finding reconciliations to be possible in all cases." The commission had really recommended no-grounds divorce or divorce by demand, rather than simply no-fault divorce; but the commission had also advocated a mandatory screening process which was intended to safeguard against impulsive divorce by informing people of the availability of counseling services. As it has turned out, the trial courts have applied the new law so as to allow divorce on demand, *McKim* notwithstanding, but the legislature eliminated the conciliation program which had been intended as a countervailing force.

No-fault represents a significant change in divorce practice, but it has been surprisingly well received, both by the public at large and the legal profession. Sidney Traxler, a Beverly Hills attorney, states that there "was a little problem with acceptance at the beginning, but now all the judges and lawyers in this state who are experienced in this field endorse the concept of divorce without fault one hundred percent." Even those like Harry Fain who object to the mechanics of the statute that was adopted do not advocate a return to fault divorce. There is a sense, however, that no-fault may not be the final step. Tim Savinar says, "People saw through the old circus where there was a lot of screaming back and forth, so the legislature came up with no-fault. But they didn't really go the full way. Certainly my clients see through the circus of going in and just saying 'yes–yes–yes–yes–yes' in order to get a divorce."

Finally, no-fault divorce does make a difference. The most obvious one in California has been the increase in the number of divorces. Richard Dinkelspiel says, "There was no real problem in getting a divorce before the new law was enacted. The grounds of 'extreme cruelty' could be most anything." Yet tens of thousands more people are getting divorced under the new law than did under the old, a fact which indicates that there is something about the way fault divorce appears, rather than the way it may really be, that deters some people from formalizing the end of their marriage.

It is this statistic, the increase in divorce in California, that is most often pointed to in other states where no-fault divorce is being debated. Opponents claim it proves no-fault undermines family stability, while advocates say it only shows that many unhappily married people have been unshackled from the hypocrisy and unfairness of the former system. As important as the increase may be, it unfortunately has obscured other effects of the new law, such as the virtual elimination of perjury, the resulting respect for the legal system, and, perhaps most important, a reduction in the trauma of divorce for the people involved.

California was the first state to abolish completely fault-based divorce; consequently its experience has been carefully scrutinized by others contemplating divorce reform. Yet no-fault divorce can take many forms; for example, concrete proof of marital breakdown may be demanded or marriage counseling may be made a prerequisite for all divorce actions. Hence what has happened in California may not necessarily be a good guide to what will occur if it is adopted elsewhere.

# Chapter Three

# No-Fault in Other States

By 1972 five states — Iowa, Florida, Oregon, Michigan, and Colorado — had followed California's lead, abolishing all the fault-based grounds for divorce and replacing them with a marital-breakdown standard. But each state introduced its own variations.

Iowa's new law, which went into effect in 1971, allows divorce if "the legitimate objects of matrimony have been destroyed and there remains no reasonable likelihood that the marriage can be preserved." Essentially this is the same test originally proposed by the Governor's Commission on the Family in California, and, at least in theory, it may be superior to the "irreconcilable differences" formula ultimately adopted there. It is less ambiguous in that a judge cannot deny divorce unless he finds a "reasonable likelihood" of reconciliation, not just a remote chance. Perhaps people might differ as to what the "legitimate objects of matrimony" are, but in practice this has raised no problem. In the first year and a half under the new Iowa law, reportedly only one divorce was denied. As in California, no-fault divorce has become divorce on demand in practice. Unlike California, however, Iowa requires a ninety-day cooling-off period and compulsory counseling before a divorce can be granted.

Florida adopted an "irretrievable breakdown" of the marriage test in 1971; it also preserved, probably unnecessarily, mental incompetence as a second ground. The Florida law also made sweeping changes in its provisions for alimony, described in

Chapter Four. Oregon's no-fault law, which became effective in 1972, was patterned after the California statute, hence is subject to the same criticism that irreconcilable differences could conceivably mean different things to different judges.

California, Iowa, Florida, and Oregon all made broad revisions of all aspects of their divorce laws; but Michigan took a different tack, changing only the grounds for divorce and leaving untouched the traditional rules regarding alimony and custody. Thus Michigan has a no-fault standard for divorce (modeled after Iowa's) but still freely admits evidence of marital fault for all collateral issues. This apparent inconsistency was the by-product of compromise. The legislature requested the Michigan Law Revision Commission to draft a reform bill and the commission proposed comprehensive changes in the laws. The organized bar, however, felt that the proposed revision was poorly thought through and recommended that marital breakdown simply be added to the traditional fault grounds, such as adultery and cruelty. The commission balked at the idea of having fault and no-fault grounds coexisting in the same divorce statute. "Although this allows parties to use the more honest and less traumatic approach, it does not guarantee that they will do so. To have a statute allowing both approaches creates a philosophical inconsistency which is difficult to justify."

Ultimately the bar was willing to go along with the abolition of all fault grounds and the commission agreed not to press for more extensive reform. George Snyder, who was chairman of the Family Law Committee of the Michigan State Bar Association at the time, states, "We weren't sure then that drastic surgery was necessary, but there is something to be said for tidiness; perhaps our proposal was a little complicated. In retrospect, the bill as passed was a sound piece of legislation."

Part of Michigan's new no-fault ground provides that "An admission by the defendant of the grounds for divorce may be considered by the court but is not binding on the court's determination." In other words, if a wife suing for divorce alleges that the marriage has broken down and the husband concurs, the court is not compelled to believe them. Some people read this clause as a signal that no-fault divorce in Michigan was not going to be divorce for the asking, and at the outset there was doubt about how the new law was going to be interpreted. Several judges in one county were reportedly intending to continue to require proof of fault to establish marital breakdown; in fact, there was some fear that the new law might be harsher than the old. A legal scholar noted that "one can imagine a judge, whose commitment to the institution of marriage is deeper than that of the immediate parties, denying a divorce for a single act of adultery, cruelty, or desertion, even though he would have been bound under the old law to grant a divorce upon a showing that such a marital offense had been committed. Instances may well arise where the judge denies a divorce when both parties want it, simply because he feels a breakdown has not occurred." There was also concern that a conservative judge could find that the marriage had broken down, but still deny the divorce by ruling that there was a reasonable likelihood of reconciliation.

Snyder says that for the most part such fears have not materialized. "The act has appeared to work generally as the legislature hoped it would, that is, assuring that a divorce will be granted when requested by one party." There have been a few cases in which trial judges have denied divorces, but these have been the exception, not the rule. Although most cases do come to the same result, judges handle them in different ways. Those who had been hardliners under the old law tend to require more evidence of breakdown than others who are simply satisfied with one party's statement that the marriage has fallen apart and cannot be saved. If the spouses have been separated for any appreciable time and one of them is adamant that the marriage is dead, divorce is almost always granted regardless of the personal predilections of the judge who hears the case.

There has been no official study of the impact of no-fault in Michigan, but Snyder reports that an informal poll indicated an increase in the number of divorces in 1972, the first year under the new law, of roughly ten or fifteen percent. Some of this rise might be attributed to people who had considered filing for divorce in 1971, but waited until the new law went into effect. Snyder discounts this explanation, however, as the statute was written so that it would apply retroactively to pending cases. He thinks that the adoption of no-fault has changed many people's attitudes about divorce. "The publicity that was given enactment of no-fault in Michigan had an effect on people who previously accepted their lot and were 'gutting it out,' so to speak. The idea of having to make public accusations against the other party dissuaded some individuals, and there were couples who didn't get along, but thought they didn't have grounds under the old law. The popular belief is that divorce is now much easier. There are no statistics on this, of course, but in our own office, we've noted a new feeling — people say they want to get a no-fault divorce."

Colorado implemented a comprehensive reform of its divorce laws in 1972, but some lawyers there feel the new no-fault ground, "irretrievable breakdown of the marriage," should have been added to the old grounds rather than completely replacing them. Howard Rosenberg, chairman of the Family Law Section of the Colorado Bar Association, generally favors the provision which was enacted, but does note that, as elsewhere, there has been some disagreement about its meaning. "There is ambiguity as to what a judge can do where both parties — or just one of them — alleges under oath the marriage is irretrievably broken. We have some judges who are saying, 'Well, it's just like it used to be. I still have the right to determine if the marriage is dead,' and parts of the statute seem to support that view, but another section says the judge *shall* find the marriage is broken unless the evidence shows otherwise, so there has been a lot of trouble in determining the proper role of the court."

Homer Clark, who teaches law at the University of Colorado, states that "The judges I've talked to, with one or two exceptions, indicate that the effect of the no-fault provisions is to give a divorce to everybody who wants one. But there are a couple of recalcitrant judges. One I know of asks if the marriage is really broken by criteria which remain a mystery to me. He denies some divorces, but not very many."

The Colorado legislation is based on portions of the Uniform Marriage and Divorce Act, a model bill approved in 1969 by the National Conference of Commissioners on Uniform State Laws and subsequently amended by them. The commissioners have no power to compel the enactment of any of the model statutes, but they are a well-respected body, so revisions which they suggest ordinarily carry substantial weight within the legal profession and in state legislatures. The Uniform Act was drafted by a committee of legal scholars, practitioners, and social scientists from various parts of the country; but the final version has a definite California flavor, being in many respects a hybrid of what was originally proposed and what ultimately was adopted there.

In the eighty years the National Conference of Commissioners on Uniform State Laws has functioned, every one of their bills has been routinely endorsed by the American Bar Association; as the A.B.A. is a much better-known organization, its endorsements have given the commissioners' proposals added clout. But beginning in 1970 and continuing into 1973 the A.B.A. has deferred action on the Uniform Marriage and Divorce Act, a stand which has generally been interpreted as a rejection of no-fault divorce. Most of the opposition within the A.B.A. has come from its Family Law Section, some of whose members are suspected of acting out of fear that no-fault divorce will ultimately mean no-lawyer divorce. The section has endorsed no-fault "in principle," but until it supports a concrete proposal, this may be an empty gesture. If the A.B.A. ever does endorse the Uniform Marriage and Divorce Act, or any other formulation of no-fault divorce, it is likely that a number of states will adopt it quickly. In the middle of 1972 Nebraska and Kentucky scrapped the traditional fault grounds and substituted marriage breakdown grounds. Similar legislation is pending in most other states, though the chances for passage in the near future vary widely.

Although the various marriage breakdown statutes which have been adopted so far differ somewhat in their wording, they all share common problems, the most apparent of which is ambiguity: what indeed is marriage breakdown and how is it proved? Critics of the new laws say that they ought to provide guidelines or definitions for breakdown, but draftsmen are reluctant to spell out specific kinds of misbehavior as symtomatic of breakdown for fear that it would invite the very fault evidence, pigeonholing, and adversary procedure for which the current system has been criticized. For example, one section of the new English law, which went into effect in 1971, purports to make irretrievable breakdown of marriage the sole basis for divorce, but the following section states that a judge cannot hold that the marriage has broken down unless there has been proof of adultery, cruelty, or the like. With one hand the law abolishes fault divorce and with the other it resurrects it. To avoid this result, most American breakdown statutes have been deliberately vague, though some have been more so than others. This has led to some initial confusion as to what it takes to prove marital breakdown sufficiently to get a divorce, and this confusion has caused concern that the new laws might be applied unevenly, as each judge could theoretically apply as strict or loose a rule as he pleased.

In practice, however, this has rarely been the case. Marriage breakdown may not really be a triable issue. Most conservative judges, who hope to get to the heart of marital problems to discover if they can be overcome, apparently have a hard time declaring that the marriage has not broken down, if either the husband or the wife insists that it has. This has led to an ironic result. Advocates of marital-breakdown statutes contend that they do away with the artificially narrow and unrealistic fault categories and replace them with a meaningful inquiry into the actual state of the marriage. The former is true, but the latter generally is not. Although the statutes may have been conceived to give judges more flexibility, in both directions, to decide if divorce is appropriate, they have been applied in such a way that divorce can be had for the asking.

In theory a marriage-breakdown standard could be devised which would allow the court to make an independent inquest into the state of the marital union instead of just relying on the parties' own assessment of the marriage; however, there are several obstacles to doing so. Perhaps the most compelling objection is the need to protect individual privacy. The fruits of a penetrating inquiry into the most intimate details of a marriage relationship might not be worth the price. There is also a dilemma in respect to the test the judge should apply for breakdown: if the statute spells out specific criteria, as England's law does, there is the danger of indirectly returning to a mechanical fault approach; yet if a more subjective standard is used, there is a risk that it will vary from judge to judge. On balance, it seems wise simply to rule that the marriage has broken down if one of the parties says it has. In effect, this constitutes divorce on demand. The marriage-breakdown laws are praised for doing away with the hypocrisy of the fault system, but they themselves might be criticized for meaning one thing in theory and another in practice.

New Hampshire, Idaho, North Dakota, Texas, and a few other states have taken a halfway step toward no-fault divorce by adding a breakdown test to their old lists of fault grounds. In Texas, for example, adultery and cruelty are still grounds for divorce; but divorce may also be granted if the marriage has become "unsupportable because of discord or conflict of personalities that destroys the legitimate ends of the marriage relationship and prevents any reasonable expectation of reconciliation."

Herma Kay, among others who have written on divorce reform, has been critical of this mongrelization of fault and no-fault grounds. She assets that "if a divorce is to be granted because of breakdown, proof of fault is simply irrelevant. If, on the other hand, proof of an unjustified and unforgiven wrong act is sufficient to terminate the marriage in law, inquiry into whether the marriage has ended in fact is unnecessary. The two approaches cut in different directions; seeking opposite goals, each relies on different facts."

The objection to having fault and marriage-breakdown grounds together in one divorce statute is not simply one of philosophical elegance. Where the old grounds are retained, there is a danger the traditional notions of fault will be carried over and applied to the breakdown cases. New Mexico, Alaska, and Oklahoma have had "incompatibility" as a ground for a number of years. It would seem that incompatibility could be proven without having to establish who was responsible for it, but the continued existence of the fault grounds on the books makes it hard to convince many judges and lawyers in those states that incompatibility means just what it says. For the most part courts there have interpreted the term strictly, refusing divorce where a husband and wife simply do not get along with each other and have required that incompatibility be proven with evidence which could just as well support a finding of cruelty. One court went so far as to deny a divorce after it conceded that the husband was incompatible with the wife — it was not convinced that the wife was incompatible with the husband. Walter Wadlington, who teaches law at the University of Virginia, believes that the general ineffectiveness of the incompatibility grounds should serve as a warning that a no-fault ground should not be grafted onto an existing fault-divorce statute. "Regardless of legislative intent, many courts simply cannot conceive of eliminating fault from consideration without an unequivocal legislative mandate to that effect, and perhaps not even then." He also notes that, "If incompatibility were given a truly non-fault interpretation, it probably would preempt most other grounds for divorce. On the other hand, the preservation of such fault-oriented defenses as recrimination frustrates the apparent legislative intent that the addition of incompatibility as a ground should serve the purpose of dissolving hopeless marriages."

Texas tried to avoid this problem by specifying in its statute that the determination that the marriage has become unsupportable is to be made "without regard to fault." The new law also abolishes the defense of recrimination and limits condonation. As a result, the great majority of petitions for divorce in Texas are based on unsupportability; there are no official figures, but some lawyers estimate that ninety percent of all cases are brought under the no-fault ground. Louise Raggio, the former chairman of the Family Law Section of the Texas Bar Association, says, "Where both parties say the marriage is unsupportable, that is usually enough for divorce; but there have been a handful of trials where one person, usually the wife, contends the marriage is still supportable. A few divorces have been denied where the marriages are of long standing and the separation has been short." There is no waiting period in Texas — a man can walk out of his house one night and sue his wife for divorce the next morning — so some judges are reluctant to grant divorces automatically.

Tacking a no-fault ground to an existing statute may be the only politically feasible way of accomplishing divorce reform in some states, but it does have shortcomings. Even if judges and lawyers can be persuaded that marriage breakdown is indeed something different from cruelty, the general public may understandably be confused as to what it takes to get a divorce. As long as some people continue to get divorced under the old system, the problems of bitterness, hypocrisy, and unfairness will persist, at least to an extent.

Marriage breakdown and incompatibility are not the only kinds of no-fault divorce. In fact, another form of no-fault divorce has existed largely unnoticed in the laws of some states for more than a hundred years. In addition to the traditional fault grounds, almost half the states allow a couple to divorce after they have been separated for a specified period of time. These "living apart" statutes vary in wording and, more important, in their interpretations, from state to state, but most allow a couple to get a divorce simply on the basis of physical separation. In theory, that the husband and wife have lived apart for the required time is taken as conclusive proof that the marriage has broken down. As the family has already dissolved, severance of the legal bond does not seem to be a threat to society's interest in preserving the marriage. In a sense divorce based on separation may be a more radical notion than marriage breakdown, for it allows a person to dissolve his or her marriage without even a *pro forma* investigation by the court.

Rhode Island, hardly a hotbed of avant-garde concepts of marriage and divorce, has had "no-fault" divorce since 1893. Several limitations, however, have kept Providence from being a serious rival for Reno's divorce business. Until 1972 the Rhode Island separation statute required the husband and wife to live apart continuously for ten years before either could apply for a divorce; the period was recently cut to five years. A judge still has the discretion to deny divorce, though it is hard to imagine a couple, separated for half a decade, that has more than a freakish chance of reconciling.

The separation periods required by most statutes vary from one to five years, but because most people are not willing to wait so long, they resort to alternatives, even if they require perjury or travel to another state. In order to make a separation ground more realistic, many legislatures have cut the time requirement significantly. Texas, for example, reduced its requirement from seven to three years, but that is still far too long a delay for most people.

The development of separation as a no-fault alternative has been hindered by the fact that it has always been appended to the traditional grounds, almost as an afterthought. In no state is separation the only basis for divorce. Just as in jurisdictions which allow divorce for incompatibility, courts inject fault notions into what is actually a no-fault ground. For example, the North Carolina law purports to allow divorce "on the application of either party, if and when the husband and wife have lived separate and apart for one year. . . ." There is nothing in this statutory provision requiring that both parties must have agreed to separate, but the North Carolina courts allow "abandonment" to be raised as a defense. Thus a woman who leaves her husband for a year is not permitted to get a divorce against his will. He, however, may divorce her. This limits the availability of the ground and the lack of mutuality raises the same adversary and bargaining problems inherent in fault divorce.

New York's statute specifically limits the separation ground to situations in which the parties have both signed a separation agreement or have been separated by a court decree. The latter, legal separation (sometimes called separation from bed and board or limited divorce), can be ordered only if the complaining spouse can prove specific grounds, just as in divorce. The limitations imposed by the New York law prevent living apart from being used unilaterally. A person cannot leave home, then ask for a divorce based on separation unless his or her spouse will sign an agreement or consent to a judicial decree. If either of these conditions is met and the one year has run, the husband or the wife can ask the court to convert the separation into divorce; this will be done automatically, provided that the petitioning party has substantially conformed to the terms of the separation.

This limited type of no-fault may seem modest, but it represents a giant step forward for New York, which until 1966 allowed divorce only for adultery. Since then matrimonial filings have increased fourfold, with the majority of cases being brought under the separation or cruelty grounds. Just as the increase in California divorces after no-fault can be partially attributed to a decline in Nevada's, the rise in New York is in part due to the fact that many New Yorkers are now getting divorced at home instead of out-of-state. In the middle nineteen-sixties, tens of thousands of New York citizens received Mexican divorces, but, since then, that country's laws have been severely tightened. Other countries like Haiti and the Dominican Republic have tried to fill the void, but migratory divorce is only a trickle compared to what it once was.

New York also abolished the traditional defenses to divorce, such as condonation and recrimination, with one interesting exception. Henry Foster, who was influential in the enactment of the new law, states, "We deliberately retained the defenses in respect to the adultery ground in order to discourage its use. A husband has a hell of a time winning a divorce in New York on the basis of adultery, so people use other grounds."

Although New York's law was revised quite recently, there has been considerable pressure for still further change. As one lawyer put it, "Our new law brought New York from the Stone Age all the way up to the nineteenth century." A number of bills have been introduced into the legislature which would make marriage breakdown the sole ground for divorce. Foster expects that in the relatively near future New York, and most other states, will adopt a totally no-fault approach.

Until more extensive reform comes, there will be some attempts by New Yorkers who want to divorce and remarry immediately to get around the one-year waiting period established by the separation statute. Some jet to the Caribbean for a quickie divorce, but Max Rheinstein thinks they could accomplish the same thing by staying home. He notes that the statute requires the separation agreement to be in existence one year before it may be converted to a divorce, but because it need not be notarized at the outset, there is no way for a court to know when it really was drawn up. He suggests that "parties who do not mind a little lie may 'execute' their agreement today in the morning, dating it as having been made one year earlier, 'subscribe and acknowledge' it before the notary in the afternoon, and commence the action for divorce the next day. Since there is no oath involved as to the correctness of the date of execution, no perjury is committed." If he is right, people willing to follow this procedure would not have to wait a year to get a divorce, but merely the time it takes to get the case before a judge. Foster states, "Theoretically, the date could be fabricated, but I have never heard of any phony filing."

Separation statutes do not necessarily eliminate the perjury associated with fault divorce. If a couple wants a divorce immediately, they may be able to lie about how long they have lived apart. As a practical matter, most divorces are preceded by separation; hence this may be less of a problem, particularly if the statutory period is reasonable. In a contested case, of course, the party who does not want the divorce can try to convince the court that there has not been an adequate separation. Otherwise the court has no way of verifying that fact, unless the law provides that the couple must register their separation in some way at the outset.

In 1971 New Jersey added separation for eighteen months to its grounds for divorce; until then they had included only adultery, willful desertion, and extreme cruelty. Richard DeKorte, the Assemblyman who sponsored the bill, said, "Our basic notion was to provide for a reasonable and rational end for marriages, rather than forcing people to create cases to fit into our three pigeonholes." Almost everyone was surprised by how quickly the impact of the new law was felt. Mortimer Neurnan, the clerk of the Superior Court in Trenton, had to hire more employees just to handle the added paperwork. "The new law opened the door pretty wide and people are rushing to take advantage of it. But to tell you the truth, I had no idea there were so many people out there who wanted to get divorced."

In the first twelve months the statute was in effect, the number of divorces in New Jersey went from fifteen thousand to more than twenty-five thousand, an increase of almost seventy percent. Opponents of divorce reform use such statistics to try to prove that no-fault undermines family stability, but a closer look indicates that this may be a misreading of the New Jersey experience. What is noteworthy is not that so many people wanted to get divorced, but that so many were immediately able to satisfy the requirement of being separated for a year and a half. Most of the people who divorced after the revised law went into effect used the separation ground, and all who did so had to be living apart from their spouse long before the new ground was available. Many had been separated for five years or more. Rather than encouraging people to split up, no-fault in New Jersey simply permitted legal termination of marriages which were already long dead. It might be argued that even though the first wave of divorces cannot be attributed to the law, the more lenient grounds will cause people to separate in the future; but this seems unlikely, given the eighteen-month requirement which should deter impetuous decisions.

Monsignor Aloysius Welsh, a spokesman for the Catholic Church in New Jersey, publicly opposed the bill when it was debated and continued to criticize it after it went into effect. "What they have now is the cart before the horse. The thing that should have been done was an in-depth study to find out what the reasons were for the break-up of a stable marriage." Such a study might be appropriate if the contemplated standard for divorce had been marital breakdown, but where the standard is separation for a year and a half, the death of the marriage should be apparent. Studying the causes of marriage breakdown might produce valuable information for social scientists, but like an autopsy, it would not do much for the particular corpse being examined.

Some legal scholars believe that separation statutes are the best way to implement no-fault divorce; to be effective, such laws should require only a reasonable period of living apart, perhaps a year or even less. Moreover, either spouse should have the right to ask for divorce, regardless of who might be more to blame for the marriage breakdown and resulting separation. As the experience in New Jersey and other states shows, when the separation ground is made more reasonable, it is used much more frequently. In time it could virtually supersede all the other grounds, even if they were still retained on the books.

In 1972 Vermont quietly adopted what may be the most progressive separation statute to date. It provides for divorce "when a married person has lived apart from his or her spouse for six consecutive months and the Court finds that the resumption of marital relations is not reasonably probable." The six-month period is the shortest in the country. Although the judge does have some discretion to deny a divorce, he can do so only by finding that reconciliation is "reasonably probable." In that event, he can order a sixty-day continuance and may suggest marriage counseling, but to date this has rarely been done. Most judges take the position that if one person says he or she is not going back under any circumstances that eliminates any reasonable probability of reconciliation.

John Williams, the chairman of the Family Law Section of the Vermont Bar Association, says that the new law has been an overwhelming success. "Other than residency, Vermont was always a liberal divorce state, but there was a lot of obvious lying and hypocrisy. One of our problems was judge shopping. There were a couple of Catholic judges who didn't make things very easy, so most lawyers would avoid them by waiting until the next term they were not sitting."

Under the old law most divorces were based on "intolerable

severity" which was equivalent to mental cruelty in other states. It still exists as a ground, but according to Williams, the separation provision is used almost exclusively. "The judges frown on using intolerable severity, and there really is no point in doing it, unless perhaps you really do have grounds and don't want to wait six months, but I haven't had any such case."

The enactment of the Vermont law received virtually no attention nationally either in the public press or within the legal profession. Even many people in Vermont, including some lawyers, are unaware that divorce is now available on demand, whether or not there is a contest. Williams himself states that he does not think that Vermont "will ever go as far as California," but in many respects it already has. He does not believe the divorce rate has gone up appreciably in Vermont and explains this by the liberality of the former law. "Divorces were easy to get if people were willing to lie, cheat, and steal, and, perhaps unfortunately, most of them were." It may be too early to make a final assessment; when people recognize the extent to which the law has been changed, it may begin to have a more noticeable effect.

Separation statutes are certainly preferable to the traditional fault approach, but they do have certain drawbacks. One is interpretation. What constitutes separation and when does it begin? Military service, long hospitalization, or a temporary job in another area can force a couple to separate, even though they do so with no thought of ending their marriage. If, while they are apart, one of them decides to get a divorce, should he or she be able to claim that, for the purpose of the statute, they have been "separated" from the last time they saw each other? At least until now, most courts have required that the time be established when the couple recognized their problems and did not expect to reconcile them. Judges have a great deal of leeway to decide the point at which this was reached in each case. If separation is to be given greater emphasis as a ground for divorce, there should be guidelines so that the law is applied uniformly; however, these can be difficult to draft.

The most serious shortcoming with living apart as a ground is that it can discourage efforts at reconciliation. A couple that has been separated for several months may toy with the idea of getting back together, but their lawyers will warn them that if reconciliation fails, the separation clock is turned back to zero and the time they have already spent apart will not count toward divorce. The risk of dragging out the unhappiness longer than is minimally necessary deters people from trying to work out their problems together. For example, a couple who had lived apart for ten months in a state requiring a year's separation might well not want to chance an attempt at reconciliation if it meant that it would take still another full year— instead of two more months— to get divorced should their efforts fail.

The lawbooks are full of cases in which judges have tried to determine how much actual physical separation is needed to satisfy the statute, and generally they have taken a mechanical approach. The problem is not easily solved by rewording the law, because any significant concession which allows people to try to reconcile also undercuts the basic premise of the separation ground, that is, that a certain period of living apart demonstrates that the marriage has broken down. The more interrupted the separation period is, the less can be inferred from it.

Goldstein and Gitter criticize separation statutes for forcing a husband and wife who want a divorce "to assume the extra and often intolerable financial burdens of two abodes. . . ." They contend that this is economically discriminatory. "Advocates of enforced separation as 'proof' of marriage breakdown must have in mind an image of the suburban husband who can go live at his club or his city or summer residence for a few weeks while awaiting a divorce. For many people, especially the poor, there is simply no place to which they can temporarily retreat for an enforced separation." Two houses are more expensive than one and are thus a burden most couples can hardly afford, but Goldstein and Gitter seem to overlook the fact that this is a permanent problem, not a temporary one. Few people who are in the midst of getting divorced still want to live together, so the separation statute itself does not impose any extra economic burden.

As stated earlier, separation grounds may be more radical in conception than marriage-breakdown statutes, but, because they have existed in the laws of so many states for many years, they may seem safer and more familiar to legislators. Cutting the separation period from five years to one and eliminating the fault defenses, like condonation and recrimination, may seem less threatening to conservatives than adopting a breakdown standard. The Uniform Marriage and Divorce Act was introduced in the Vermont legislature, but got nowhere, while the new separation provision passed with relative ease. On the other hand, that separation has cohabited with the fault grounds for so long has tended to color it with fault notions in many jurisdictions. Marriage breakdown is a cleaner break with the past, thus may offer a better chance of ridding the divorce system of its archaic qualities.

Thus far in this country no-fault divorce has taken the form of marital-breakdown, incompatibility, and separation statutes; but there are other proposals which in some respects may be superior. Goldstein and Gitter view divorce as a strictly private matter to be resolved by the adults involved. "The court should not be empowered to deny divorce because one spouse or a child of the marriage objects. Granting divorce, even over objection, best serves the state's goal of maximizing individual freedom. Denial of divorce means that both parties, though no longer a viable marital unit, are denied the freedom to establish meaningful new as well as residual family relationships." They contend that because the state has no power to compel people to wed, it has no business forcing people to stay married against their will.

Explicit divorce by demand has been adopted in other countries, most notably post-revolutionary Russia, but that history is not likely to recommend its adoption to state legislators in the United States. Many people are uncomfortable with openly allowing a person to end a marriage regardless of the wishes of his or her spouse. The picture of a seventy-year-old man leaving his wife of fifty years for the proverbial chorus girl is not an appealing one, but in many ways it is a red herring. Under the present divorce system, especially under existing no-fault laws, such a man can make good his escape. If he lives in a state that still employs fault divorce and his wife will not consent to one, he can and probably will make her miserable. It is the situation which is unfortunate, not the availability of divorce.

It might be argued that it is "easy divorce" which makes old men chase after chorus girls, and no doubt our attitudes about marriage reflect in part our practices in respect to divorce. But to believe that stricter divorce statutes can in some paternalistic way help us have happier marriages by making us walk the straight and narrow is to give too much credit to law and too little to biology. This is not to say that divorce by demand would have no effect on the dynamics of marriage, for it would constitute a major departure from the fault system. By contesting a fault divorce one person often can preserve at least the legal shell of his or her marriage, while divorce by demand permits his or her spouse to end it unilaterally. On one hand this might make marriage more volatile by increasing the potency of threats to walk out of the marriage. Sanford Katz, the editor of the *Family Law Quarterly*, believes that divorce on demand would tend to cause people to run away from their problems rather than solve them. Perhaps this is true, but not all marital problems have solutions and walking out can sometimes be a healthy response. Giving each partner the right to end the marriage might help people address the issues at stake, that is, not whether they can get divorced, but whether they should.

Any divorce law, whether by demand or otherwise, should provide for a reasonable waiting period in order to discourage hasty decisions. Even the Muslim practice that allows a husband to end his marriage by telling his wife, "I divorce thee," makes him say it three times, not just once. For example, a divorce by demand law could require a person who thinks he or she wants a divorce to register that intent with a clerk of the marriage bureau of the local city hall. If the person reappeared several months later to confirm his or her intent, the divorce would be granted automatically. Collateral disputes could be litigated if necessary, but the divorce itself would be just a matter of registration. Perhaps if there were minor children or if the spouse objected, the period could be somewhat longer.

It is curious that divorce by demand has so little political support, because it is not really much different from what is already practiced under the marital-breakdown statutes which have been enacted. Similarly, divorce based on separation is divorce by demand in some states, though usually with a longer waiting period. The difference between divorce by demand and no-fault divorce as it is practiced is one of degree and appearance rather than kind, and in most instances, even these differences have been slight.

Yet divorce by demand is not politically palatable. The original legislation proposed by the Governor's Commission on the Family in California would have given judges no discretion to deny divorce, but its supporters were careful to describe it as marital-breakdown divorce, not divorce by demand, which it really was. Apparently there is something disquieting about the word "demand." "Request" might be milder, but even then it may remind us too starkly that divorce can be had for the asking. We are more comfortable when a court grants divorce after finding that there are irreconcilable differences, even if that finding is based solely on the fact that one spouse demands a divorce.

Revising our marriage laws offers a different, more imaginative approach to divorce reform. For example, a bill has been introduced in the Maryland legislature which would permit three-year marriages which either party could dissolve without going into court. There have also been proposals to make the process of marrying harder by setting more stringent minimum age and waiting requirements or by making premarital counseling mandatory. Some of these proposals require radical changes in our attitudes about marriage, while others require substantial government spending on family services. These kinds of alternatives are discussed more extensively in Chapter Ten; at this point they seem unlikely to be adopted in the near future. So long as it is easier to get a marriage license than it is to get a driver's license, a high frequency of marital problems is inevitable. If we choose not to change our marriage laws, then our divorce statutes ought to reflect marriage as it really is, not as it ideally might be.

# Chapter Four

## Alimony

No one likes alimony. Not the men who pay it, nor the women who receive it. But men are louder in their complaints; until recently, most women suffered silently. S. William Klein, a New York stockbroker, was so enraged by his treatment in the divorce court he helped found Alimony, Ltd. (now called Fair Divorce and Alimony Laws), an organization with thousands of members dedicated to abolishing alimony or at least strictly limiting it. Klein says, "The minute you hear the judge sentence you to alimony, you join a fraternity of crippled men."

The fraternity's common bond is misery, its dues are paid to ex-wives, its ostensible purpose is to reform the laws; but its principal pastime seems to be swapping stories about the unfairness of the divorce system. Whenever the brethren gather, they tell of the man who supposedly paid alimony faithfully for thirty-two years, then missed one payment and was hauled into court by his former wife. Or of the prisoner on death row at Sing-Sing who was ordered to pay his wife thirty dollars a week. They gripe about an unnamed woman in Chicago who supposedly uses her twelve-thousand-dollar-a-year alimony to keep herself—and her lover—in a luxurious lakeside apartment. And they curse the judge who awarded ninety-seven percent of one husband's income to his ex-wife.

It is not clear if any of these stories are true, but the men who tell them swear that they are. The recurring theme in them all is that the courts discriminate against men. Nathaniel Denman, an engineer who founded Family Law Reform, Inc., in Massachusetts and has been associated with similar groups in other states, says that the fundamental problem with divorce law throughout the country is that it is biased against men. "Men in divorce are treated almost as badly as Negroes who tried to vote in the South in the thirties — that's no exaggeration."

Alimony payers like Denman have a love-hate attitude toward the law. They are bitter about what they think it has done to them, but at their meetings or in their literature, they love to rattle out legal jargon to support their opinions: "forcing a man to pay alimony when the marriage contract has been terminated is 'involuntary servitude' "; "family court judges flout the 'equal protection clause' of the Constitution"; "imprisonment for nonpayment of support is 'cruel and unusual punishment' "; "making the husband pay the wife's attorney's fees violates the 'equal rights amendment.' "

Harry Seifert, a former president of Alimony, Ltd., says, "New York's divorce law sees a husband as an opponent to be clobbered. He is a bounder who plans to leave his wife and kids shivering and unprotected in the storms of life. By contrast the wife is treated with slobbering sentimentality. As the law sees it, the attorney's primary purpose is not to support a needy wife, but to punish the husband."

There are even some women who believe that the system ties a millstone around the necks of men who have to pay alimony. Deborah Ziegler and her husband both work; he pays alimony to his first wife, who does not. The present Mrs. Ziegler resented this situation and, as a result, founded The Other Woman, Ltd. Her group got off the ground with the publication of an advertisement which asked, "Send us $1 to help get your ex-wife a job. Or a husband." Under the headline was a cartoon depicting the supposedly typical ex-wife, sitting in front of a television, munching chocolates. Married women like Deborah Ziegler who are members of The Other Woman, Ltd., and similar groups object to the way their husband's alimony drains their family income; single members complain that their men friends who are divorced refuse to marry them because they do not want to support two households.

Members of such organizations are sensitive to the charge that they are traitors to their sex, hence they are quick to contend that alimony is also destructive for the women who get it; they say that it stifles women, both socially and professionally. "So many of them turn to rage and anger," states Mrs. Ziegler. She points out that because an ex-wife receives alimony only if she remains single, there is an economic penalty imposed on a divorced woman who remarries.

It is hard to separate fact from fiction in this kind of criticism. Alimony is the last vestige of a marriage which very likely ended in misunderstanding and bitterness, and, as such, it is a lightning rod that attracts all the residual hostility. Often the husband and wife try to use alimony to punish each other. It is not surprising that when people discuss alimony, there is more heat than light shed on the subject.

Nevertheless, dissatisfaction with alimony is not limited to embittered men (and their women friends) who do not like paying it. Henry Foster, of New York University Law School, believes that the alimony system rests on archaic assumptions. "Many of our decisions on support and alimony issues reflect an uncritical commitment to an economic system and status which no longer exist. The image seems to be that of the abused housewife of the early 1800s rather than the competent and employable and perhaps self-sufficient modern woman." He says that it is our "blind acceptance of rules fashioned in earlier times and under different circumstances" which keeps us from addressing what he feels are the critical questions. "Does alimony perpetuate dependency or continue antagonisms which make readjustment difficult if not impossible? Does alimony engender resentments and hostilities on the part of the man, or in the alternative where he has a guilty conscience, does it serve as a penance which absolves him of guilt?" Because these questions have been largely overlooked, they have no definitive answers.

Judge Samuel Hofstadter of New York has been outspoken in his criticism of the way that alimony is awarded. "Alimony was never intended to assure a perpetual state of secured indolence. It should not be suffered to convert a host of physically and mentally competent young women into an army of alimony drones, who neither toil nor spin, and become a menace to themselves and a drain on society." Although the judge has often stated that alimony is proper for a woman who has remained "vocationally dormant," as he puts it, during a long marriage, his phrase "alimony drone" has made him a favorite of those who oppose alimony and a foe for those who support married women's rights.

Corinne Grad, a member of the Older Women's League in New York, believes that the "drone" stereotype is untrue. "There's a whole smokescreen of women in the antialimony group who make it appear that women receiving alimony have been married only a few months, have no children, and sit and watch television and eat chocolates all day." As "demeaning" and "destructive" as alimony may be to women, there is strong justification for its existence, at least given the present social structure in the United States. In most marriages the husband is the principal wage-earner. Even if the wife works (and a great many do), financial matters are usually left to the husband; in many states, this is by rule of law, not just custom. Women liberationists are fighting for a new basis for marriage, one of true partnership with shared control over family income and property; but, until that is achieved, divorcing women will face severe handicaps. Often they have sacrificed their careers to be housewives, have accumulated no savings, and are burdened with the custody of small children.

Betty Friedan has stated that "the reality today is that most wives — because of unequal treatment in the past — are not equipped to earn adequate livings for themselves or their children." Clare Booth Luce and Florynce Kennedy, women with radically different political philosophies, agree that alimony or some similar compensation should be considered a basic right, not charity. Mrs. Luce, herself once divorced, believes that, "In view of past services — often worth many thousands of dollars — rendered as domestics, women should be given severance pay." Ms. Kennedy compares marriage to slavery—"You work, but you don't get paid on any guaranteed, agreed basis. You're dependent on your husband's largesse." As a consequence she thinks that alimony should be considered "in terms of reparations."

Although many women feel alimony is necessary, they are not necessarily happy with the present system. Their principal objection is that alimony is paid only sporadically. Foster has concluded, "It is not uncommon for husbands or ex-husbands not to pay at all or to be in arrears in over 50 percent of the cases. A study in Gary, Indiana set the figure at 89 percent of the cases." He interprets nonpayment as proof that alimony and child support awards "often are unrealistic and economically and psychologically unsound." As a solution he urges that pre-trial procedures allow a husband to tell his side of the financial story in a non-oppressive atmosphere. It is not simply the orders which disturb most men, but the way they are made. Foster describes the "sense of outrage engendered by bargain counter support orders in some of our metropolitan centers, where the husband, who has his side of the story, is not allowed to air his grievances, and has a support order jammed down his throat." Perhaps it should not be surprising that many men express their resentment by refusing to pay.

Herma Kay points out another dimension of the problem. "Apart from the isolated but well-publicized cases of generous allowance, which may be motivated by tax considerations, alimony awards in general have been found insufficient to support the ex-wife adequately and are notoriously difficult to enforce." Homer Clark has stated that rather than being excessive, "the major difficulty with alimony has been the reverse: It usually cannot be granted in sufficient amounts to support the wife and children adequately." A study in a lower-income area of Boston showed that the median amount of yearly support due from the husband was only $1,638, a fraction of what a family needs to subsist; even this amount can be hard to collect. Sixty-one percent of the judges who responded to an American Bar Association survey said they usually awarded less than thirty-five percent of a husband's net income as child support, even though it takes tens, perhaps hundreds, of thousands of dollars to raise a child to maturity.

The traditional way of trying to compel payment of alimony and child support is threat of jail. Failure to live up to a judge's decree may be contempt of court. Although debtor's prisons are thought to be an institution of the past, many states still have alimony jails. In recent years criminal nonsupport has been the fifth most frequently prosecuted crime in Massachusetts. A Vermont man who owed his family twenty-five hundred dollars in temporary support was found in contempt of court and served more than five years in jail. After he was finally released, the state indicated that it was considering imprisoning him again unless he paid the additional twenty thousand dollars which had mounted up while he was in jail.

There is sharp disagreement about the utility of making non-support a crime. Some people claim that prison sentences are a necessary deterrent. According to their view, a man who spends several months in a cell is likely to be more careful about making his payments in the future; and, more important, his imprisonment will serve as an example for dozens of others. Many judges take a stern view of a man who seems to have shirked his familial responsibilities. One Massachusetts judge thinks that jail is the correct solution. "Three months in the house of correction never hurt anyone."

There are many people who disagree. They point to the fact that even with the threat of jail hanging over their heads, many men fail to keep up their alimony and support payments. In part this laxity may be because the law is applied unevenly; judges differ widely in their attitudes toward punishing nonsupport. For example, some Massachusetts counties have percentages of non-support convictions twice as high as others. Moreover, the percentage of those convicted who are actually sent to prison varies by fivefold.

Stricter application of the law is not the answer, however, since prosecution is expensive both for the people involved and for the state. In some areas, welfare agencies try to instigate court action against delinquent fathers in order to reduce public assistance to their families, but most offices are so swamped with work that they are unable to handle all the cases. The family, in turn, may find it far easier to collect a regular welfare check—even if it is smaller—than to try to track down a father who has fallen behind in his support payments. Furthermore, imprisonment is an expensive method of enforcement. Once a man is in jail, he certainly cannot earn enough money stamping out license plates to make up what he owes; it costs the state more to keep him locked up than it would to support him and his family in a welfare program.

The specter of prison adds more hostility to situations which are already brimming over with bitterness. In 1960 the *New York Times* reported that a Stanford University psychologist, who was not identified, had studied eight hundred women who were responsible for having their former husbands jailed. "His findings were that 70 percent of these women were suffering from 'psychoses bordering on sadism.' " That the study is anonymous may make its precise results suspect, but there can be no doubt that any woman who feels it is worthwhile to put her former husband in prison must be a desperate person. There can also be no doubt that on the husband's release he will feel vindictive, not contrite, and so the post-marital warfare will escalate. Alimony creates resentment among the men who must pay it or risk jail, it fails to support most of the women who receive it, and attempts to enforce payment are often futile and always expensive. In sum, alimony does not work.

One of the basic problems is a lack of agreement about what alimony is supposed to do. The term derives from the Latin word "to nourish," reflecting the husband's traditional duty to provide for his wife and children. But in those states where marital fault is still the basis for divorce, alimony also is used to punish the wrongdoing spouse. Anthropologist Paul Bohannan states, "In most states, the amount of alimony is more or less directly dependent on whatever moral or immoral conduct of the wife may come to the attention of the court. A woman known to be guilty of anything the court considers to be moral misconduct is likely to be awarded less than an 'innocent' wife. The law varies widely on these matters; practice varies even more."

The statutory and case law of some states specifically requires that alimony be punitive. In New York a woman's marital misconduct, if it constitutes grounds for divorce, bars her from recovering any alimony, even if her husband was also at fault. Louisiana refuses alimony if the court finds that the husband and wife were equally responsible for the death of the marriage. Regardless of the written law, judges have broad discretion in making alimony awards, and their own attitudes often show through. In every state there are judges who are reputed to favor men, as well as others who are supposedly sympathetic to women. A recently divorced Massachusetts man complained, "The courts don't treat people equally. Given two men with the same circumstances, they can end up with different orders, even though they earn the same amount of money and have the same number of kids." Before Florida recently changed its alimony law, Judge C. Pfeiffer Trowbridge chided some of his colleagues for having an unrealistic view of marriage problems. "Male promiscuity and female virtue have long been the adult version of the nursery rhyme of what little boys and girls are made of."

Some people still believe that alimony should be used as a fine levied against a promiscuous husband or a reward for a wronged wife. Eli Bronstein, a New York matrimonial lawyer, thinks alimony should depend on who was at fault. "If a woman has been a tramp, why reward her? By the same token, if a man is alley-catting around town, shouldn't his wife get all the benefits she had as a married woman?" To agree with Bronstein, you must be confident that the judicial system can determine who really was at fault for the breakdown of the marriage. As discussed in the first chapter, it is probably unrealistic to attribute blame solely to one person; and, in any event, courts are not equipped to conduct a meaningful inquest into the death of the marriage. Putting an economic penalty on fault encourages suspicion and makes it worthwhile to hire private detectives who may turn up some damning evidence against the other spouse. Rather than fostering reconciliation, alimony based on fault makes it profitable for one of the spouses to push for divorce. Fault-based alimony also is biased against women in that it offers them nothing but the status quo (that is, continued support) to win and everything to lose.

On the other hand, alimony laws sometimes discriminate against men. Many states will not order a woman to pay alimony to her former husband no matter what the circumstances are. A New York engineer who was unemployed asked for seventy-five dollars a week alimony from his ex-wife who was earning ten thousand dollars a year teaching. The judge refused to grant him anything, commenting that a husband's proper role is to support himself "out of his property or by his labor" and that a "husband who looks to his wife for support is placed in an unnatural relationship." The judge happened to be a woman, but it was not a case of a judge sticking up for her own, as New York's statute specifically refers to men as the payers of alimony, not the recipients. There has been pressure in New York to give men the right to be supported by their former wives if the facts warrant it, but any reform will have to be legislative. The Georgia Supreme Court recently upheld the state's statute which makes alimony an obligation that only men owe women, not vice versa, in spite of a challenge that such a provision was unconstitutional.

The confusion about alimony goes beyond what alimony is for, to what it really is. If a man says he is paying one hundred dollars a week in alimony, he is probably including in that figure sixty dollars in support for his children. But when a woman says that she refuses to take any alimony from her ex-husband, she seldom means that she does not want his help in paying the expenses of raising their children. A newspaper which reports that a movie star has had to pay his former wife "a million dollars in alimony" is usually speaking of a one-shot division of marital assets, not on-going payments of support.

Even the separation agreement and the court's decree may not be definitive. Most of what the husband must pay after divorce may be termed "alimony" so that he can deduct it from his taxable income, even though the parties themselves think of the money as going to the children; the tax consequences of divorce raise intricate strategies in the negotiations between the husband and the wife. Similarly, if the husband agrees to call most of his payments "alimony," he may soon be free of his obligation if his wife remarries. But if she does not, he will be saddled with large payments long after their children have grown. Haggling over the fine points of a financial settlement can consume days of lawyers' time and as a result, hundreds, sometimes thousands, of a family's dollars which could be better spent on its own needs.

In some ways the distinction between alimony and child support is often artificial. When a woman receives her monthly check, she does not budget a certain fixed part for herself and the rest for the children, because most of the costs of running a household, like rent and grocery bills, are not easily divisible. There are other financial problems at the time of divorce, such as division of property — who gets the house and so forth — but as most families accumulate relatively little capital, alimony and child support are usually the crucial issues.

How then does no-fault change alimony and other financial matters? In some cases, not at all. Michigan's new law made breakdown of the marriage the sole ground for divorce, regardless of fault; but it did not change the old criteria for determining alimony. The Michigan statute directs the court to consider, in addition to the capacities and resources of the husband and wife, "the character and situation of the parties, and all the other circumstances of the case." Most judges have construed "other circumstances" to include the conduct of the parties, particularly their roles in the breakdown of the marriage. Eliminating consideration of fault from the grounds, but not from the financial issues, is somewhat inconsistent. It permits the granting of divorce on a more realistic basis, but it fails to eradicate the acrimony and name calling from the proceedings. It seems necessary in terms of hard cash for both the husband and the wife to try to make the other look immoral and undeserving.

George Snyder, who practices law in Detroit, has noted "an increase in the number of cases which are tried on the matter of finances, apparently because the old inhibition against trying these issues has been removed." Under the fault system, alimony and child support are often agreed to before the hearing as part of the bargain to get an uncontested divorce. Now that it is a "practical impossibility," according to Snyder, to stop a spouse from getting a divorce in Michigan, one person can no longer use the threat of a contest as a tool for extortion. "Previously, one or the other party would decide that they had better settle the economic disputes in order to remove the risk that there might be no divorce, but now people are more willing to let the dice roll with the judge."

If the evidence were limited to the needs and means of the people involved — as opposed to marital misconduct — the fact that financial issues are now tried in open court might lead to arrangements which would be more willingly accepted and observed by the parties. But to the extent that Michigan courts still try to fix the blame for the breakdown of the marriage, the process of divorce will reinforce the hostilities between the spouses, rather than temper them. Money is often at the heart of the dispute. If a reward is given to a person who can prove that his or her spouse was at fault, divorce will be made more bitter than it has to be, and that bitterness will very likely carry over into the post-divorce relationship. The husband may refuse to pay the alimony and support, the wife may retaliate by bringing him into court, and the judge may have to hear the same case over again.

In California, divorce reform was much more extensive. Alimony is now called "spousal support," which is free of the pejorative associations of the old term and introduces the concept that it can be paid by either the husband or the wife. The new law instructs judges who are determining the amount and period of payments to consider "the circumstances of the respective parties, including the duration of the marriage, and the ability of the supported spouse to engage in gainful employment." The new standard is primarily one of need of the supported person and the resources of the former spouse. In California, "circumstances" are strictly economic, and marital fault, which was a factor under the old alimony law, is no longer relevant.

Wendell Goddard, a young lawyer, surveyed a number of California judges to determine the effect of the new law. Although the increasing cost of living together with varying circumstances makes comparisons difficult, he has concluded that "There is some evidence which suggests that the Act has accelerated the growing tendency among judges to award a wife less support, both in duration and amount." Judge Spurgeon Avakian of the Superior Court of Alameda County has pointed to another reason for the apparent trend in California. "Changing social attitudes about divorce and about employment of women have, in reality, been reflected increasingly in the courtroom, where it is often expected that a wife not encumbered with small children should contribute to her own support. . . . The increasing emphasis on equality for women is incompatible with the idea of lifelong spousal support from an ex-husband." There are more than thirty million working women in the country, almost three-fifths of whom are married and living with their husbands. Judges in California and elsewhere are beginning to believe that many women need not be completely dependent on men.

As mentioned earlier, California's courts can order a woman to support her former husband. A judge in Sacramento awarded one man thirty thousand dollars a year in spousal support, and, as a property settlement, he also received one of the two family homes, three thousand shares of General Motors stock, a country club membership, and various incidentals. His wife was heiress to the Kool-Aid fortune and he apparently had never worked. Tim Savinar, a San Francisco lawyer, had a more mundane case. "The husband was on welfare, but the wife was a computer programmer. I said to the court, 'Look, this guy is unemployed. He's got skills, but there's no market for them now. She's making a good income, so she ought to contribute.' And the judge bought it. But that's very rare." That it is still unusual for a court to order a woman to support a man does not mean that judges are reluctant to carry out the intent of the new law, but that men are ordinarily able to work themselves.

Unless the couple agrees otherwise, the new law requires judges in most cases to split the marital property equally, regardless of fault or, for that matter, need. In California there are basically three kinds of property in a marriage — his, hers, and theirs; it is the latter which is equally divided. Under the old law judges had discretion to give more than half the community property to the wife if the husband had been accused of adultery or cruelty. Goddard observed that one result of the changed law has been "the reduction of hostility caused by disputes over property. Under the prior law, the plaintiff not only sought to establish that she was entitled to a divorce, but she was also forced to describe every affair, attack, or unkindness of the defendant in order to increase her property award. Such contests engendered bitterness between parties and among friends and neighbors who were called as witnesses."

Most families accumulate so little property that there is not much to haggle over; even where there is wealth, the fact that the judge must order a fifty-fifty split if the couple cannot agree on some other division greatly limits the room for bargaining. When cases go to trial the issue is who owns what and how much is it worth, rather than who is the more deserving, though as mentioned earlier, some lawyers try to sneak in evidence of fault in order to sway the court's sympathies. There can be exceedingly technical questions of valuation where the property includes good will of a business, pension plans, stock options, and the like, but this was true previously.

In some instances, the inflexibility of the new law can be unfair. It is possible, for example, for a man or woman to have a great deal of personal wealth, none of which the law considers marital property; such assets cannot be reached by the other spouse regardless of his or her need. Kathryn Gehrels, a San Francisco attorney, states that the new law can work hardship on women, because after separation, the husband can treat his earnings as nonmarital property but still have the right to manage the community property. "The husband can exhaust the community property for his living expenses and put his income in the bank. If it's a year or so before the case comes to trial, the husband has built up his own nest-egg, but there is no community property left for the wife." Judges can make some adjustment of these kinds of inequities, however, by altering the amount and length of spousal support.

In respect to financial matters, the new California law departs from traditional divorce policy in two significant ways. By having support a question of monetary need rather than moral reward, the statute moves closer to making divorce a termination of an economic partnership, as opposed to a remedy to correct supposed marital wrongs. Most observers in California believe that the removal of fault from money issues has diminished hostility in many divorces, at least to an extent. It may be impossible, of course, to prove this conclusively, as hostility is a quality which may elude measurement. It could be argued that such laws will tend to cut the other way, that is, that a husband whose adulterous wife has caused him emotional agony may feel even more enraged when he learns that the court will not even hear evidence about her behavior. If he feels that the court's support order was not based on all the facts, he may resent paying anything to his wife.

The idea of requiring a man to pay alimony to his adulterous wife offends many people. Snyder claims that in Michigan "the visceral reaction of the bench and bar is overwhelmingly that the relative conduct of the parties and the marital history should and will continue to be a factor in property, alimony, and other financial matters." It may be tempting to take a righteous attitude, but this is unwise given the difficulty in ascertaining who really was to blame for the marital problems; on balance it seems better to shut the courtroom door to marital fault. In time, this may mold public opinion so that marriage is regarded as involving certain economic rights and obligations which exist regardless of fault.

The second change, the equal division of marital property, also reflects a conception of marriage as an economic partnership; but it has proved to be more troublesome. The law can be harsh if the husband has a productive career ahead of him and the wife has none because she has sacrificed her economic future for the well-being of the family. In such a case, an equal division of the tangible marital property does not truly reflect what each spouse has put into the marriage and what each is taking out. In this respect, the flexibility of the Michigan law may be superior. As Snyder notes, "A pat formula probably works an injustice in a majority of cases. Divorce is the last place you should have a standard solution or routine procedure. Personal matters require flexibility." Flexibility does have a cost — it might be expensive to determine a truly equitable division of property and precautions would have to be taken to prevent some judges from basing their decisions on subjective impressions of fault; yet overall such an approach seems superior to the arbitrary division practiced in California.

The provisions of the Uniform Marriage and Divorce Act differ somewhat from both the California and Michigan statutes. The act gives judges some leeway in dividing what it calls "marital property" — it need not be a fifty-fifty split. A judge must determine the contribution which each spouse made to the property, as well as the present economic circumstances of the parties. A court can also award "maintenance" payments to either spouse, but only if that spouse lacks sufficient property for his or her needs and is unable to support him- or herself. In deciding the amount of maintenance, the judge is to consider the length of the marriage, the standard of living which was enjoyed, the ability of the person paying maintenance to meet his or her own needs, and the time necessary to train the person receiving maintenance for employment.

The stated purpose of these provisions is to "encourage the court to provide for the financial needs of the spouses by property disposition rather than by an award of maintenance." In theory, this is a sensible approach, as it would be far simpler to resolve the economic problems of divorce with one lump sum payment, rather than by a series of monthly installments which may spread over decades. Yet few couples acquire sufficient assets to provide for the future needs of the residual family, which in most instances includes a mother and minor children. Usually some sort of child support and spousal maintenance is the only viable solution. Most women do not have any property of their own to speak of, are limited in their employment prospects, and are burdened with caring for young children. Although the Uniform

Act purports to limit the court's power to award maintenance, as a practical matter, most divorced women would still qualify for it under the standards it establishes. By no means does it abolish alimony, but by basing it on the needs and resources of the parties, rather than their alleged fault, it represents a major step forward over the present law. While it could not neutralize all the hostility which emerges during the negotiations about money, it probably would moderate it.

The new Florida divorce law, which abolished all fault grounds, also included a provision which many judges have interpreted to limit a woman's right to alimony. Many have subscribed to the position of one judge that henceforth "Alimony is to be considered rehabilitative, not as a lifetime pension." There is an increasing belief among the Florida judiciary that alimony is not only a burden for men, but it can also debilitate the women who receive it. Instead of putting a woman in a position where she must rely on a dole from her former husband, judges are limiting alimony to getting her back on her feet so that she is economically self-sufficient.

This approach seems progressive, but in practice it has created problems. Many women are unable to work, either because they are physically incapacitated or are untrained for available jobs. Rehabilitation is not always possible, particularly for an older woman. Nevertheless, some judges have taken a harder line than was probably intended by the legislature. For example, one Florida woman who had been married for twenty years and suffered from phlebitis was granted only enough money to cover the costs of raising her teenage son. As for her own needs, the judge told her to find a job where she could stay off her feet. A young woman with a child was refused enough money to cover her final year in college. The judge justified his denial on the ground that she had not completed college while she was married, nor was she willing to remain married and go to college, an offer her husband had made. The implication of the decision seems to be that a woman who desires a divorce over her husband's objection may sometimes forfeit rehabilitative alimony.

There has been disagreement with the legal profession in Florida as to what the new law means. Some judges have virtually abolished alimony, but according to Virginia Anne Church, a

Clearwater attorney, there are others who "are going on with business as usual and continuing long-term or reduced alimony." The statute still permits marital fault to be considered in respect to financial questions; a wife's adultery may be an automatic bar to her receiving alimony. Eventually the Florida Supreme Court may provide sufficient guidelines so that the new law becomes clearer, but for the first several years, at least, it has created a great deal of confusion.

Some Florida trial judges have gone so far as to terminate alimony in divorces which were granted years ago, even though both parties had agreed to lifelong alimony as part of their bargain to get divorced. Women who thought they had a permanent source of income are suddenly discovering that it has been turned off or at least cut down. Divorced men from other states are starting to move to Florida with hopes of getting their alimony agreements revised. In 1972 Judge Francis Good of Massachusetts was asked by a woman for an injunction to prevent her husband from getting a divorce in Florida. The couple had been legally separated in 1968 and at that time the husband had been ordered to pay twenty-two hundred dollars a month in support. Depending on which side of the case was to be believed, either the husband had moved to Florida or he was just commuting there for weekends. Judge Good made it clear that he did not like the idea of using the laws of one state to "supersede and subvert" the laws of his own, but he concluded that he had no power to stop the husband from going to Florida to reopen the case, if he established satisfactory domicile there. Similar situations are occurring elsewhere, and it is becoming apparent that the impact of Florida's new law will be felt far beyond its own boundaries.

States like Florida, New Hampshire, Pennsylvania, and Texas, which allow no alimony or have drastically cut it, may have found a cure which is worse than the disease. It may make life more comfortable for divorced men, but it is unrealistic to think all that women need is just a little push from the alimony nest. Indeed, some can learn to fend for themselves and rehabilitative alimony is appropriate for such women. Yet many others are unable to support themselves fully, perhaps because of age, responsibility for young children, or job discrimination. Louise Raggio, a Dallas attorney, states that no-fault has created a new poverty class in Texas. "We have no alimony in our state. Just the thought of alimony puts fear in the hearts of Texas men. So middle-aged women are getting dumped out of marriages without a cent. If there is no community property, they end up being supported by their children." The Family Law Section of the Texas Bar Association has been trying to win acceptance for a "readjustment allowance," to be awarded to the nonworking spouse upon divorce, but thus far has not succeeded.

To abolish alimony is to externalize the cost of divorce: society picks up the expenses through welfare and aid to dependent children, previously borne privately. It has been suggested that child-rearing is an occupation providing benefits both to the family and to society at large, and as such, it should be salaried. The question is, who pays? Most taxpayers have a less than generous attitude about welfare programs, so, as it becomes more apparent that a reduction in alimony often leads to a corresponding increase in welfare payments, there will be public support for retaining the present alimony system, as ineffective as it may be.

The alimony problem may have no satisfactory solution. Representative Robert Drinan and many other family law authorities believe there is simply not enough money to go around. "The greatest myth in all of divorce law is surely the illusion that a man can form a second family while giving 'support and maintenance' to the children of his first marriage. Men even in the upper and middle class can hardly finance two homes." While he was Dean of Boston College Law School, he found that a third of the students applying for scholarships were basing their need on the fact that their fathers were supporting two households.

Whatever support figure is reached, it probably will be either too much from the husband's point of view or too little from the wife's. Homer Clark has stated, "Legal principles devised by Solomon and administered by Oliver Wendell Holmes could not mitigate the hardship caused by divorce to families in the middle- and lower-income ranges. The hardship is made even more acute when the husband remarries, as he frequently does, and acquires a new family to support. In that event an income barely adequate for one family must be stretched to provide for a husband, a wife, an ex-wife, and two sets of children."

Though there are no panaceas, a number of positive steps

might be considered, in addition to eliminating marital fault as a factor in financial questions. Wisconsin requires any divorced man who wants to remarry to go to court to prove that his children are not likely to become public charges as a result. Usually the court considers only whether the man is presently paid up, but in many instances it is only after remarriage that the serious financial problems come to a head; thus the Wisconsin requirement does not actually guarantee that payments to the former family will continue to be made after the second marriage. Those men who are already behind in their support can try to circumvent the law by marrying out of state, though some have been prosecuted for doing so. The biggest weakness of the law is that at best it can only prevent remarriage and that does not insure that the children will be supported. Many divorced men have no thought of re-marrying. The law does, however, have a symbolic value in under-scoring the difficulty of trying to finance two households at one time.

Tightening collection procedures is probably a more fruitful avenue for reform. The National Organization of Women (NOW) has proposed that alimony and child support obligations be de-ducted from a husband's paycheck just as taxes and union dues currently are. Such a system would impose the cost of collection and distribution on the employer, but this could be assessed to either the husband or the wife. At present, a great many resources, both public and private, are wasted in inefficient and ineffective efforts at enforcement. It would be far cheaper to pay a modest collection fee than to resort to the expense of court hearings and alimony jail. Divorce decrees are already a matter of public rec-ord, so such a system would not be an unwarranted invasion of a man's privacy. Alternatively, support payments might be made directly to the court or through some social agency. The idea of automatic deductions may raise the hackles of men who do not like the idea of paying alimony in the first place and further resent the suggestion that they would not honor their obligations, but once such a system was made a matter of course, it would very likely be far less painful for everyone concerned. Senator Samuel J. Ervin, Jr., of North Carolina has proposed legislation which would make nonpayment of child support a federal crime; a national law might alleviate some of the jurisdictional problems which have made enforcement so difficult.

Could financial matters simply be left to the parties? The popular press has given a great deal of attention to marriage contracts, agreements drawn up by a man and woman before they wed, but such documents do not seem to solve the alimony problem. To the extent that such contracts help the parties define their expectations and illuminate areas of potential conflict, they may help to build a more realistic foundation for a marriage. But the magazine articles explaining "How to Write Your Own Marriage Contract" often give the misleading impression that all provisions of the contract will be enforceable by law. In fact they often are not. If a court will not recognize the contract, its terms are only as effective as the good intentions of both people, and these may be sorely tested in times of trouble.

Most states allow a couple about to marry to execute mutual contracts to will their property in a particular way at death, but agreements to divide property and provide support in the event of divorce are not enforced. Laws could be written to make such contracts binding, but they probably should not be. Dealing with problems of divorce before marriage permits negotiation in an atmosphere free of rancor, but this advantage is more than outweighed by the fact that no couple can foresee what their needs and resources at the time of divorce would be, whether it is three years or thirty after the marriage. An agreement which seems perfectly reasonable at the outset could easily become inappropriate due to change of income, increased wealth, or sickness. Even if the terms proved to be satisfactory to both husband and wife, there is no guarantee that the children's interests would have been protected as they should be. Unfortunately most problems of divorce cannot be resolved until they arise.

Divorce insurance is one of the most novel solutions for the alimony problem. Homer Clark mentioned the idea several years ago. "We are accustomed to protect families against the economic hardship caused by death, and similar hardship is caused by divorce. Why should not the same protection be authorized by statute when the family is broken by divorce?" Other scholars have referred to divorce insurance in passing, but it really has been the work of one person, New York lawyer Diana DuBroff, which has brought the idea to light. Her frustration with the present system led her to create NOISE, the National Organization to Insure Support Enforcement, which is lobbying hard to make divorce insurance available in New York and other states.

Mrs. DuBroff believes that insurance is particularly necessary for middle-income families, whose economic difficulties she feels are often overlooked. "Even they end up on welfare, because they soon find out they can't support two homes. The wage-earner, it's almost always the husband, gets driven into another state and it's too much trouble for the wife to try to chase him. So she tries to handle two or three jobs, the children are left alone, and it ends up with me defending the mother against charges of neglect." Insurance offers the double advantage of providing a lump sum when it is most needed, while eliminating all the problems which usually go with enforcing payment. "Theoretically you could do the same thing with a savings account or a trust fund, but you have to remember human frailties. There would be an awful temptation to use the money for other purposes."

Mrs. DuBroff does not conceive of insurance as a total substitute for alimony and child support, but as a device which would provide a certain basic amount to cover the family's needs, particularly the children's, during the transitional period when the economic crisis is at its peak. "During this period the woman would have the chance to be retrained. She can't think of herself as a dependent person, just because she was once married—that's got to be forgotten. It doesn't pay for her to go to court to get a five-dollar increase in support. Chasing alimony can be destructive. Ultimately some women will be able to get better jobs than others, but anything is helpful in building self respect."

The most frequent objection she hears to her proposal is that people literally will not buy it. Couples are not likely to be thinking about divorce before they marry, but Mrs. DuBroff says they should be, if not for their own sakes, then for the sake of their prospective children. "When you buy a car, you don't plan on having an accident, but the state makes you buy insurance. The statistics show there are a lot of collisions. You have to insure yourself — and others — against that possibility. It's the same way with divorce, and it's the children who really need the protection."

New York State Senator Donald Halperin has called for an

official study of divorce insurance and believes that the legislature may be willing shortly to approve its sale on a voluntary basis. This might provide valuable experience for working out the details of future systems, but it would not be a long-run answer. The very people who would fail to buy it are those who are least likely to have made some other provision for their children. A mandatory system would present difficulties, however, the most important being its legality. The United States Supreme Court has indicated that marriage is a basic civil right, so a state might not be allowed to make expensive divorce insurance a prerequisite for marrying. Senator Halperin has suggested that, as an alternative, divorce insurance could be publicly funded, possibly through Social Security or income taxes. "In the long run it would not cost as much as it might seem initially, as we would be saving money on aid-to-dependent-children payments under the welfare system."

Although no insurance company has yet issued policies or computed rates, Mrs. DuBroff does not think the cost would be prohibitive. It is true that the number of divorces annually is rapidly approaching one million, but that represents only a small proportion, perhaps two percent, of existing marriages. The ultimate chances of a marriage ending in divorce may be calculated as high as forty percent, depending on what figures are used, but the probability of a marriage ending in any particular year is actually rather low, two percent or less on the average.

Senator Halperin has encountered no formal opposition to the proposal, but has heard the objection that insurance might stimulate divorce by making it financially attractive. "You have to recognize that there are conflicting public policies: you don't want to encourage divorce, but you want to be sure children are properly fed, clothed, and housed." He thinks that this objection can be overcome if the insurance also provides a benefit for those couples who manage to stick together. "After the parents pass the childbearing age, and the children go off on their own, the money could be transferred into life insurance or something more accessible, like a retirement pension or education fund. That way people wouldn't feel that they had lost money by staying married."

It is too soon to know if divorce insurance is feasible, either economically or politically. Some people might regard it as a jinx and others might resent sharing the cost of other people's irresponsibility. There also might be objection to the idea of insurance companies' profiting from what would be in large part a forced savings plan. Conceivably, the availability of insurance might force a family in desperate financial trouble to separate in much the same way that families are now forced to separate in order to maximize welfare aid to children. Mrs. DuBroff herself does not promise that she has the final answer. "As long as I've made people think, as long as they recognize that the present support system is a hoax, I've performed a function. If my idea is no good, then people should come up with a better one."

The role she is playing in divorce reform may eventually prove to be larger than she has imagined. Up until now most of the emphasis in revising the divorce laws has been directed at removing fault from the grounds or changing court procedures; where alimony and child support have been considered, reform has been only to the extent of how it should be measured, not the manner in which it should be paid. By dealing directly with the fact that most alimony and support orders are inadequate and loosely enforced, Mrs. DuBroff has gone to what is often the heart of the dispute, both during and after divorce. If the financial matters can be resolved, the other problems may easily fall into place.

Senator Halperin is wary about associating divorce insurance with broader attempts at reform at this point. "No-fault and divorce insurance can be connected very neatly, but if the people or the legislators aren't ready for no-fault, I would hate to see divorce insurance go down with it." If he can keep the two proposals separate and if insurance or some other scheme proves workable, Senator Halperin and others like him may have come upon a relatively uncontroversial solution to one of the most hotly contested aspects of divorce.

# Chapter Five

## Children

In most divorce courts, children are seldom seen and never heard. Nevertheless, most of the marriages in the United States which end in divorce involve families with minor children. The husband and wife may know what they want and be able to hire lawyers to help them get it; but no one speaks for the children, even though they have at least as much at stake in the divorce as do their parents. The adults are most likely to be preoccupied with their own problems and to be in a position where what is best for them is not necessarily best for their children. Moreover, the emotional stress during the last days of a dying marriage can be such that the parents do not really know what is best for themselves, let alone for anyone else.

Almost by default the courts have been given the responsibility to see that children are not the innocent casualties of matrimonial warfare. If the children have been injured by the conflict between their parents, the court is expected to heal the wounds. Unfortunately it rarely does.

Twenty years ago Dr. J. Louise Despert, the author of *Children of Divorce*, concluded that "The parents, divorced or divorcing, who take unresolved problems concerning their children to court in search of a wise solution will rarely find it there." To a large extent, her observation is as true today as it was then. More than a third of all divorces in which there are children are followed by further litigation, most of which directly involves them. Many former spouses continually refight the old issues of who should have custody of the children, how they should be raised, and how much each parent should contribute to support. Others must turn to the courts to try to get their former spouses to live up to the judge's original decree.

A father who has lost custody of his child may spy on his ex-wife to see if she is guilty of some immoral behavior that would convince a court to reverse its decision. A woman who is angry — rightly or wrongly — with her former husband can get back at him by denying him his visitation rights. Both of these tactics can lead the couple back into court. If a parent who has lost a custody battle is truly desperate, he or she will snatch the child from the spouse and take it to another state in the hope that the court there will take a different view of who ought to keep the child. Even in those divorce cases where there is no further court action, there is always an element of uncertainty, and it is the children who seem to suffer most from it.

Much of the criticism of the way the law treats custody problems is premised on unreasonable expectations. A judge who must decide a custody case can only make the best of a bad situation; he cannot guarantee a child all the advantages which it would enjoy in a stable and loving home. Divorce is often the least harmful of the available evils, but it is never the best of all conceivable worlds. Even if we realize that a judge's choices are limited, we often expect him to be clairvoyant. His custody decision is really a prediction that one parent will be better for the child than the other, but children and their needs grow and change, as do the abilities of parents to fulfill them. No matter how much a judge discovers about an individual's past, he cannot be certain of his or her future. The person who on past performance seems to be the more promising parent may prove to be less able to cope with the problem of being alone as head of the household. Others who were less responsible during marriage may mature after divorce. And even if a judge could be absolutely certain how people will behave in the future, he still would face complex questions about what is good for children in general and what a particular child needs in a given case.

Determining custody is made more difficult by the tension accompanying divorce. If a couple has fought for years while married, they will likely continue to fight during and after the divorce. Sometimes the hatred is a product of a parent's selfishness or jealousy. A bitter man or woman can use a custody battle to harass his or her spouse or to extort a more favorable property settlement. For example, a man may threaten his wife with a custody contest in hopes of getting her to back down on her alimony demands, even though he has no real intention of having the children. Sometimes, however, a custody contest reflects an honest, though unfortunate, disagreement about how the children should be raised. A husband and wife who have developed deep differences in their social or religious beliefs probably will not want to leave the upbringing of their children in the hands of a heretic. Whatever the parents' motives, custody disputes are among the hardest cases judges must hear. Actually Solomon was lucky when he had to decide which of the two women was the child's real mother — if he had been a judge in a divorce court, the contesting parents might have called his bluff and forced him to slice the baby in two.

Custody cases are so inherently difficult that it is unrealistic to expect judges to find a solution in each one which ensures future happiness and fulfillment to everyone involved. There simply are no panaceas. But even when the performance of the courts is judged on this basis, it still seems less than satisfactory. Part of the problem is workload. Most family courts are confronted with an ever-increasing backlog of cases and the result has been assembly-line justice. This puts pressure on lawyers to get their clients to come to an agreement beforehand, even if it is not a very good one. The court is not bound to approve the custody arrangements the parties have made, but, as a matter of practice, it almost always does. A contested case does not necessarily get a deeper hearing than one that is not, for some judges are impatient with lawyers who take a great deal of their time. If courts often take only a cursory look at custody cases, it should not be surprising that their decisions get little respect and are frequently followed by more litigation.

The creation of more judgeships and the introduction of administrative improvements would ease the burden and allow courts to give custody cases a fuller hearing, but the family court judges must be improved in quality as well as quantity. Henry Foster contends that "If courts are to do a better job in custody matters it is essential that such cases be referred to judges who have some knowledge of behavioral science and who are receptive to expert testimony and the recommendations of specialists." When untrained judges deal with social workers and child psychologists, they tend either to react defensively by rejecting their suggestions out of hand or to embrace them uncritically. Few judges have the kind of experience that allows them to take a balanced view. Unfortunately, family court judges are generally the lowest paid and least respected members of the bench. This lack of status is unfair to a great number of dedicated and sensitive judges, but it operates as a strong factor to discourage other good lawyers from giving up successful practices to take on judgeships on family courts.

A more fundamental difficulty is that the rules and practices which have been applied to custody cases have traditionally focused more on the rights of the parents than on the well-being of the children. Until the nineteenth century, a father had virtually unfettered power over his children, regardless of the wishes of their mother. (She in fact was in much the same position as the children.) He could even sell them if that was his whim. Only in the last hundred years have women been granted an essentially equal right to the custody of their children. In fact, however, the pendulum has swung even further as the courts have usually presumed the mother to be the better custodian for young children. Only quite recently have the courts begun to view parents as having truly equal claims to the children, and also to regard the children's interest as paramount.

In theory the establishment of grounds for divorce and the resolution of custody disputes are two separate matters, but in practice much of the evidence that goes to the former is also considered in respect to the latter. As a result, notions of fault have become entwined in custody law; marital conduct is often the key to who gets the children. Until recently some states required a man who wished to have custody of his children to prove that his ex-wife would be unfit as a mother. This test of fitness first developed in cases where a nonparent, such as a grandparent, uncle, or friend, wanted to take custody away from a child's mother or father; but it was extended to apply to contests between divorcing parents. It was not enough for the father to prove that he would be a better custodian, but he also had to establish that his former wife was so irresponsible or immoral that she would actually harm the child, either physically or emotionally.

Although the fitness test is apparently going out of fashion, its legacy is still felt. Many judges persist in seeing custody cases as questions of moral right and wrong. A woman who is supposedly at fault for breaking up her family may be punished by being denied custody. The fitness approach invites judges to sermonize on the immoral conduct of the wife, rather than to examine the issue of whether the child would be better off with her, in spite of her past behavior.

An increasing number of states now ostensibly require that custody be awarded according to the best interests of the child. In theory, this standard should direct the court's attention to the central issue; but too often it has done little more than provide a legal cliché that judges can use to justify whatever decision they happen to reach. Both the fitness and best interest tests give a judge wide latitude in deciding custody cases. Most judges who still apply the fitness rule weigh fitness in terms of some of the same factors affecting the welfare of the child, and judges who use the best interest standard usually presume that it is in the child's interest to be with its mother. Henry Foster and Doris Freed have concluded that "Historically, custody awards have been dictated by amorphous platitudes or generalizations on one hand and by rigid absolutes on the other."

As a practical matter, it may not make much difference which rule is invoked; some judges speak of fitness and best interests interchangeably as if they meant the same thing. Under either test it is difficult to get a reversal of a trial judge's decision in a custody case. Appellate courts generally defer to trial judges' rulings on the ground that they heard the evidence firsthand. It takes a flagrant abuse of judicial discretion to constitute reversible error; thus family court judges have a great deal of power in custody cases.

Unfortunately both the fitness and best interest tests can exacerbate family differences rather than resolve them. The tenor of the courtroom testimony is usually negative. Each parent tries to prove that the other is incompetent, immoral, or, best of all, both. Apparently it is easier to attack someone else's character than it is to prove the strength of one's own. As a result the debate consists of charges and countercharges about who would be a worse parent, rather than who might be better. A husband who wants custody will point out his wife's every failing, real and imagined; and to defend herself, she will respond in kind. It is not surprising that many judges who have to hear this kind of testimony day in and day out finally just tune it all out.

In much the same way that the requirement of proving marital fault to get a divorce diverts the court's attention from the underlying causes of the breakdown of the marriage, the rules regarding custody can skirt what should be the fundamental question, the relationship between the child and the parent who wants custody. Under the present system children are often the consolation prizes handed out to a person who can paint a picture of martyred suffering caused by his or her spouse. Similarly, by emphasizing the adversary aspects of custody disputes, the rules reinforce the impression that there must be a winner and loser in every case. The resentments generated during a custody proceeding are bound to poison the post-divorce relationship between the parents. Worse, the children who have heard the accusations volleying back and forth can be emotionally shellshocked, and thus have trouble relating to either parent.

In some cases the question of custody is directly connected to the grounds for the divorce. For example, if a man is divorcing his wife because she committed adultery, he may claim custody on the basis that her behavior makes her an unfit mother or, alternatively, that it is not in the children's interest to be with her. Courts react to this contention in various ways. Until now Nebraska has taken a very hard line, barring absolutely a woman who has committed adultery from having custody of her children. In upholding this rule the Nebraska Supreme Court has stated that such a woman has "forfeited any right she may have had to the custody of her children because of her disgraceful conduct. One may not willfully destroy the family relationship as she has done and expect a court to give consideration to her to the detriment of the husband she has so grievously wronged." This approach punishes the wayward wife and rewards her suffering husband, but it fails to ask what would be best for the children. The elimination of fault from the divorce grounds in Nebraska may soften its custody rule.

A few states like Florida, Wisconsin, and Oregon will deny an adulterous mother custody only if her conduct directly harms the children. If she has been discrete or if the children are too young to comprehend her behavior, she will not be barred from keeping her children. The inquiry is directed, as it should be, at the quality of the relationships between the mother and the children, not between the mother and father. Most states take a vague middle ground, not always preventing a woman who has committed adultery from having custody, but in many cases placing the burden on her to prove that she will not be a bad influence on the children. Decisions ultimately depend largely on the judge's personal morality; whether he awards custody to the woman or refuses it, he can rationalize his ruling on the basis it was in the best interests of the children. Experienced family lawyers know the prejudices and idiosyncrasies of judges hearing their cases. If the lawyer for a woman who is being divorced for her adultery can see to it that the case is heard by a sophisticated judge, she may have a good chance of getting custody; if it is heard by someone else, she may lose.

The same sort of problems can arise in custody cases where one of the parents has a history of mental illness. Some courts take a more enlightened view in such cases, asking what if any bearing the illness has on the relationship with the child. Courts are generally less likely to punish a woman for having been mentally ill than for committing adultery; this may reflect a judgment that the woman did not deliberately destroy her family or disgrace her husband. Yet, Dr. Carl Malmquist has surveyed cases involving parental mental illness and has concluded that the reaction of the courts is not always predictable. "Faced with conflicting expert testimony, which a diligent lawyer can usually obtain in an adversarial setting with sufficient effort, a court may choose to ignore the experts completely or merely select those whose opinions coalesce with their [sic] own decisions based on exogenous factors or the common sense notion of the judge." Again the result largely depends on who happens to hear the case.

Trial judges have such broad discretion, it is impossible to reduce the laws and practices regarding custody to hard and fast rules. The recent trend has been away from the fitness test and toward a best-interest-of-the-child approach, but the character of custody cases has been unchanged in many respects, so that the parents are often plotting against each other when they should be cooperating as much as possible to help their children. Custody cases can drag on for years. Meanwhile, the children must live with perpetual insecurity. Much of the tragedy in custody cases is inherent in the problem; laws may be able to mitigate the harm, but they cannot eradicate it.

A state can enact no-fault divorce without specifically revising its custody laws, yet the abolition of fault grounds has a significant, though indirect, effect on custody questions. Under traditional law, a husband or wife who wants a divorce may be forced to relinquish all claims to custody of the children in order to get his or her spouse not to contest it; but if divorce can be had more or less for the asking, the other spouse can no longer use the children as hostages. Separating the issue of divorce from that of custody is an improvement. A woman who wants a divorce from her domineering husband does not have to abandon her children to him. But, by the same token, the unrestricted availability of divorce might mean that many more custody cases are likely to be fought in the courts; unless the laws are such that the cases will be decided intelligently and humanely, this could be more a loss than a gain.

When Michigan made marriage breakdown the sole ground for divorce, it left unchanged the laws relating to financial matters and custody of children. Only a year earlier, the legislature had enacted a new custody law which in effect codified much of the existing case law. It had made the child's interest paramount in all disputes and had removed the old presumption that a mother is normally entitled to custody of children of "tender years." George Snyder, a Detroit lawyer who was active in the adoption of the new custody law, states that "it has worked better than our fondest hopes." He adds, however, that "most judges still award children, particularly younger ones, to the wife. Whether this is because the judges think that's generally in their best interest, we don't know."

It may seem contradictory to praise a new law, and then to concede it has not made much difference in the outcome of cases; yet in custody matters the process, the way in which the outcome was reached may be just as important as the result itself. Even if a man still loses custody of his children, he may be more willing to accept the decision if he feels the case received a full hearing and was evaluated according to a just and consistent law.

The special commission which initiated California's new family law recommended that the rules regarding custody be changed along with the grounds for divorce. The commission was particularly concerned with custody disputes between a parent and a nonparent, though the rules which apply to such situations are sometimes extended to custody contests between two divorcing parents. The commission originally suggested moving away from the dominant parental right theory, which had required that a parent be proven unfit before a child could be awarded to a nonparent, and proposed instead using the best interest of the child as the test for custody. Herma Kay, a member of the commission, states, "This provision received more severe criticism than any other part of the draft statute when legislative hearings were held on the bill. Objections were raised that the measure reposes unlimited discretion in judges to find that the best interest of children requires their placement with outsiders even if their parents are fit, and that such discretion is likely to be abused."

While this proposal was being debated in California, the Supreme Court of Iowa unintentionally provided ammunition for those who feared that the best interest test would give judges too great an opportunity to impose their personal values in custody cases. In *Painter v. Bannister* Iowa's highest court awarded custody of a young boy whose mother had died to his maternal grandparents instead of his father, because it felt it was in the best interest of the child to be with his "stable" Iowa grandparents rather than return with his father to the "Bohemian atmosphere" of San Francisco. The judges were apparently swayed by the testimony of a psychologist who had said that the boy would likely "go wrong" if he were in the custody of his father. According to Henry Foster, the psychologist some time later admitted that he had never seen the father and that he may have "gotten carried away" during the trial, and that a complete investigation might have proven him wrong.

The spectacle of the courts' taking away the only son of a young man who had recently lost his wife in an automobile accident received national attention. Kay has stated that it is clear *Painter* "had a great impact in California and that it has given rise to many doubts about the 'best interests' standard." As a result, the California legislature rejected the commission's custody proposal and instead provided that a court could award custody to a nonparent only if it finds both that the child would be better off with the nonparent and that staying with the parent would actually be "detrimental" to the child. Kay has pointed out that this is not a major change from the old law. "The shading of difference between proving that a parent is unfit to have custody of his child and that parental custody would be detrimental to the child is a fine one indeed. To the extent that the new law is interpreted to emphasize the quality of the relationship between the parent and the child rather than the personal weaknesses of the parent, it will be a change for the better."

The new California law also creates a presumption that a child is better off with a parent than a nonparent; similarly, if the contest is between the mother and father, the mother is presumed by law to be the better parent. In both instances, these presumptions can be overcome, but only by evidence which often comes close to proving unfitness. Thus far the custody provisions of the new California law have been a disappointment. Although the statute specifically prohibits the use of evidence of marital misconduct, such as adultery, to prove that irreconcilable differences exist, such evidence is completely permissible in questions of custody. Perhaps there are no more custody fights under the new law, but clearly there are no fewer, and when custody is contested, the same bitter accusations fly back and forth. Much of what the legislature accomplished in barring fault as a factor in divorce was undone in allowing it to be considered without limitation in custody questions.

Tim Savinar, a San Francisco attorney, says that "some lawyers throw in evidence of fault to appease their clients, but most of the time it's legitimately directed at finding out where the kids should go. Then again, there are times it can get pretty ugly." After two years' experience with the new law, Alameda County Judge William J. McGuiness has complained that "Embattled parents exhaust themselves emotionally and financially in repeated contests over child custody, visitation, and support. In the process they make a public spectacle of intimate matters . . . and neither can win." He believes that people still use custody contests as weapons against their spouses or to exert pressure for a better financial settlement. "The child is caught in the crossfire of the parents' battle and in many cases judge and lawyer are oblivious to the emotional results." The relatively minor changes in the California custody laws simply have not solved the problem.

The Uniform Marriage and Divorce Act also went through a metamorphosis while it was being drafted, but its changes were in a different direction. The original draft specifically set forth the competing interests involved in a custody dispute and — much like California's law — defined certain presumptions intended to limit a trial judge's discretion. For example, the mother was to be presumed to be the proper custodian for a young child unless there were substantial evidence to the contrary. The commissioners ultimately rejected this approach and endorsed a best interest test. To avoid the criticism that the law would be an invitation to more decisions like *Painter*, the drafters included a provision which directs the court to consider "all relevant factors" in the case. These include the parents' wishes, the child's wishes, the child's relationship with members of its family, its adjustment to its community, and the mental and physical health of everyone involved.

Under traditional notions of custody law, most judges already examined such factors, but the Uniform Act did include one important innovation: "The courts shall not consider conduct of a proposed custodian that does not affect his relationship to the child." While this provision does not totally ban evidence of marital misconduct from being presented during a custody hearing, it does significantly limit it. In justifying this limitation, the draftsmen stated, "There is no reason to encourage parties to spy on each other in order to discover marital (more commonly, sexual) misconduct for use in a custody contest. This provision makes it clear that unless a contestant is able to prove that the parent's behavior in fact affects his relationship to the child (a standard which could seldom be met if the parent's behavior has been circumspect or unknown to the child), evidence of such behavior is irrelevant."

It would be unwise to bar all evidence of marital fault from consideration in child custody cases, for there can be instances in which misconduct has a direct bearing on the parent's relationship with the child; but it is important that such evidence be allowed only in those special cases. Although the Family Law Section of the A.B.A. has refused to endorse the Uniform Marriage and Divorce Act as a whole (largely because of its formulation of no-fault divorce), the Section has indicated that it would support this custody provision. Homer Clark has stated that "To the extent that marital misconduct could be used to punish a misbehaving parent by depriving him of his child, fault should not be relevant in custody cases. Parental misconduct would come to light in determining the quality of the child's relationship with each parent, but to award custody on the grounds that one parent should be rewarded or punished for parental behavior would detract from the real inquiry — the child's future welfare."

Richard Pearson, who teaches family law at Boston University, thinks the distinction the Uniform Act draws between relevant and irrelevant misconduct does not hold up. "It's difficult for me to imagine marital misconduct which would not bear on the relationship with the child in one way or another." Clark counters that it is a question of emphasis. "The same evidence may get in, but it's in a somewhat different context. In the typical case, the wife has committed adultery. I suppose most judges might say that it is pertinent to the care of the child, but more and more are saying that it is not necessarily relevant. Maybe that leaves the husband upset, but it's better than getting into the morass of proving the details of the adultery."

The less that evidence of marital misconduct is allowed, the less hostility there should be between the husband and wife, though some people like Pearson remain unconvinced that this is true. It is this hostility that Clark and others feel is "the most significant single obstacle to the acceptable adjudication of custody cases." The Uniform Act de-emphasizes fault as a consideration in custody hearings while the California law does not; in this respect at least, the Uniform Act is superior.

It may be that reform of child custody laws can be better accomplished by changing the legal procedures rather than the substantive rules. The standards for custody cause many problems, but the manner in which they are applied may be even more troublesome. There is growing support for giving any child in a divorce action his own lawyer. Custody may be the central issue in the divorce, but the children, who have the most to gain or lose, are not represented; hence the court has to rely entirely on the evidence presented by the husband and wife, though it rarely tells the whole story. Because the great majority of divorces are uncontested, the court hears testimony that is superficial, one-sided, and not infrequently false. Perhaps this charade does relatively little harm to the parents, both of whom have expressed their willingness to end the marriage, but what of the children? The court has not been presented with all the facts necessary to decide what is in their best interest, and this presumably is the appropriate test for custody.

The same problem can exist where custody is contested. A man who retains a lawyer expects him to present the strongest possible case in his behalf. If he wants custody of his children, he has the right to his attorney's undivided loyalty. His wife expects the same from her lawyer. As mentioned earlier, the confrontation of two competing interests in the courtroom should produce enough arguments and information for the judge to make a reasonable choice between them; but this adversary process breaks down if there are three different interests, and only two are represented. In a custody dispute the interests of the children may not be the same as those of either the husband or the wife. For example, if both the parents beat the children, the lawyers for the husband and for the wife may be unlikely to bring that up since it would damage each of their cases. But if such information is hidden from the court, it is unrealistic to expect the judge to act in the children's best interest.

Judge Ross W. Campbell of Michigan believes that a child's right to representation should go beyond just presenting relevant facts for the court's consideration to include the right to contest the divorce itself. He has stated that "the time has come to recognize the right of a child to continuation of its parents' marriage relationship during the period of both physical and emotional growth and development of the child until it reaches an age where separation from the parent who leaves the home will not substantially damage the growth and development of the child." Judge Campbell concedes that an exception to this principle would have to be made in cases where the continued discord between the parents is an even greater threat to the child than the break-up of the home. If both parents want divorce, however, it is hard to imagine a situation in which this threat would not be great. What child would want to live with his parents after stopping them from getting divorced? Although it is easy to agree that divorce can cause "substantial damage" to children, to contend that children have a legally enforceable right (as opposed to a moral one) to the continuation of their parents' marriage ignores the fact that some unhappy marriages are worse than no marriage at all. Love cannot be legislated, and children need loving parents, not grudging keepers.

Although a child should not be given the right to veto his parents' divorce, perhaps he should be represented in those issues which directly affect him — who should have custody, what are the proper visitation arrangements, and what provisions should be made for support. A lawyer appointed for the child could investigate the case by speaking with members of the family, as well as friends and teachers, and then advocate to the court what course would be best for the child.

Representation would have definite benefits, but it might have a very real cost. Divorce is hard enough as it is for children; putting them on center stage might be too much of an added burden. Helen Ginty was divorced two years ago, but she states that her children are still feeling its effects. "You have to understand that divorce makes children very insecure. They love both parents, but they think they are expected to choose between them. And they are terribly afraid that if they make the wrong choice, they are going to be left out in the cold. My ex-husband takes the kids one weekend a month, and they tell me that they hate him and they don't want to go. Now this worried me at first, but Ed says that when they're with him, they say that they don't want to come back to me. The kids just say whatever they think we both want to hear. It's their way of coping with the fact that their mother and father are apart. They can have it both ways. But what would happen if they had to be consistent? What would happen if a judge asked them to choose which of us should have custody? That could be really traumatic for them."

A number of judges agree, hence refuse to interview children either publicly in court or privately in chambers. They fear that if it is known that the child will have a voice in deciding who gets custody, each parent will pressure the child with threats and bribes. There is also the danger that a child will complicate the situation by trying to play his parents off against each other. Although a child should have a voice in his future, he should not have to make an outright choice until he is mature enough to handle the burdens that go with making the decision. The Uniform Marriage and Divorce Act gives a judge discretion to speak with the children in chambers, but a record of the conversation must be made available to the lawyers for the husband and wife. Opening up the record prevents a judge from deciding a case on secret, unchallenged information, but the lack of confidentiality puts the child in virtually the same vulnerable position as if he testified in open court.

Giving a child a lawyer in divorce cases does not require that he himself testify, of course, nor does it necessarily require the lawyer to do exactly what the child might want. The child's wishes should receive serious consideration, but they should not be the sole guide for custody. If the role of the lawyer is more that of an independent investigator than an advocate, much of the potential pressure on the child could be relieved.

There are, however, other objections to the proposal. Brooks Potter, a Boston lawyer, agrees that children must be protected but believes the present system already guards their interests. "I always think of myself as not only counsel for my client, but counsel for the children. Lawyers in these cases consider themselves as primarily interested in the children — the adults can take care of themselves. Remember that the more lawyers you have, the more lawyers' fees you have, and the less money will be left for family support." Potter's faith that the parents' counsel can also represent the children is typical of many family lawyers, but Henry Foster thinks it involves an inherent conflict of interest. "Counsel for the father or mother cannot be relied upon to present facts detrimental to his client to whom the duty of loyalty is owed . . . right to counsel means independent representation of the child by a lawyer who will serve his interests."

Potter contends that the conflict of interest is more apparent than real. "If I represent the mother, but after studying the facts am convinced the welfare of the children means they should be with their father, I'll tell her so. I wouldn't be honest with myself if I didn't. There have been lots of cases I've had where the father got custody because the mother just plain wasn't the proper custodian. I know pretty well the standards judges apply, and if the mother is going to lose, what's the sense in fighting it? When you have two good lawyers who know something about this field, and they work out agreements on custody and visitation, you can be satisfied that the children are well taken care of. If the wife loses custody, it means that two good lawyers — in addition to the judge — thought it was for the best, and if that's so, why pay a third lawyer to tell you the same thing?"

Potter is probably right in saying that a third attorney is not needed where the conduct of one party has been so extreme that a court would never award him or her custody. If the mother is an alcoholic who is not capable of caring for herself, let alone the children, the children may not need their own lawyer, because the attorneys for the parents may well agree that granting custody to the father is best for everyone concerned. All this assumes, however, the presence of "two good lawyers." If the lawyers are not sensitive to people's needs, the bargain they strike may not be a good one.

In most cases the issues are not clearcut. A mother may drink heavily but still be the better custodian for the children. If it is not a clearcut case, the loyalties of the woman's attorney are necessarily torn — how hard should he fight for custody? Lawyers have a great deal of power in such matters, and this makes the conflict all the more significant. Although the court retains jurisdiction over custody, a judge will usually approve as a matter of routine an agreement that the parents' attorneys have negotiated.

If the parents themselves have worked out who should keep the children, the influence of the lawyers is less important; but if the attorneys have had to twist arms to get the parents to agree, there is often resentment. Arthur Beeman has been divorced for fifteen years, but his hatred of lawyers has kept him active in divorce reform groups. "When a lawyer represents a man, he advises him not to take the children. He scares the man into giving them up. The lawyers work together under the table against the man and for the wife. They don't care what happens to the children; the next case they handle, they'll make some other deal. You think you've got a lawyer, but he's really working for the other side. He doesn't care what happens as long as he gets paid."

Beeman's description is unfair to most family lawyers, but it is understandable. Whenever two attorneys try to impose their own personal judgments on a situation — no matter how unselfish their motives might be — they open themselves up to the charge that they are selling one of the clients down the river. Providing the children with an independent lawyer also protects the parents' attorneys by freeing them fully to represent their own clients' interests.

Most proposals for representation for children in divorce assume that the court itself should appoint the attorney. This has usually been the practice in the few states where children are now represented; in other kinds of legal proceedings judges often name lawyers as guardians for minors. Judges have considered themselves the protectors of children, and, if this responsibility is to be delegated to an attorney, it might seem natural to let them make the choice. But there is good reason to be skeptical of court-appointed lawyers. Some impartial judges appoint only those attorneys they know to be well qualified for the assignment, but others abuse this kind of power and use it as a private boondoggle for their friends.

Massachusetts courts sometimes appoint lawyers as investigators in some foster care cases, and they perform much the same function as would attorneys for children in divorce. Sanford Katz, who teaches at Boston College Law School, has examined many of the reports filed by investigators and has found that their quality varies markedly. "Some people take the work very seriously and do a good job. Others spend a few hours on a case and collect a four-hundred-dollar fee. But even though the system isn't perfect, it is far better than nothing. That's why I think the same thing should be done for children in divorce."

One solution to the appointment problem, which apparently has not been tried yet, is to lessen the court's role in the selection of the child's attorney. For example, the lawyers for the parents could nominate a third lawyer to represent the children; the actual appointment could be subject to the court's approval. A more promising method would be to certify lawyers for this kind of work on the basis of their training and experience. A state agency could coordinate a system in which lawyers would be drawn from a pool. Those parents who could afford to pay for the children's lawyer would be expected to do so, but the children's right to counsel should not depend on whether their parents can afford it. Dr. Andrew Watson, who teaches both law and psychiatry at the University of Michigan, has found that "the information elicited in the course of trials involving custody is largely dependent upon the skill of the advocates, and only cases involving relatively wealthy clients receive the attention which brings forth the detailed information needed to make sophisticated judgment."

Oregon, Maine, and a number of other states already have legislation which allows a judge to appoint an attorney for a child in a divorce case, but none requires representation in every instance. Even without statutory authorization, family court judges probably have the discretion to name a lawyer for children, but it is rarely exercised; thus though a specific enabling act may not be technically necessary, the legislatures have to prod the courts into recognizing a child's need for counsel. Additionally, there must be programs which guarantee that each child has this advantage regardless of his parents' resources.

Before the new California law went into effect, Herma Kay predicted that "the introduction of a third attorney to represent the children will be less useful" where fault is abolished as a consideration in divorce. She had hoped that the mandatory conciliation proceeding, which was proposed as an important part of the reform, would lessen the hostilities of the parents to a point where they could work together for the children's well-being. Counseling was not required, however; and, perhaps as a result, custody cases in California are at least as bitter as they used to be. The mere adoption of no-fault divorce does not in itself improve the lot of the children. Unless more is done, their interests still require some sort of voice.

It may be, however, that there are already too many lawyers involved in custody disputes. Lawyers, who are trained in an adversary system to think in terms of either winning or losing a client's case, may protract the proceedings and add to the hostilities. The solution may be to remove custody problems as much as possible from the courts. Both parents could continue to share legal custody of the children and try to agree on their upbringing. If they concur that the children should live with the mother, the mother could have physical custody. When the parents disagree about some matters, as they might, they could submit the issue to an arbitrator instead of going to court.

Any arbitration procedure would have to be spelled out clearly at the start. Conceivably one person could be chosen as the arbitrator, but this probably would be impractical. Few people would want to stand alone in the crossfire between two battling parents, nor would anyone want to make himself constantly available three hundred sixty-five days a year. As a more workable alternative, the responsibility could rest with an arbitration committee made up of both people who know the child personally — such as its doctor, teacher, clergyman, and so forth — and others who have professional experience in family problems. Relying on such a committee to settle disputes has several advantages over the conventional judicial process. In most cases it would be less expensive and could be brought into action more quickly. As a result, it would have more flexibility than the courts. Additionally, the parents might have greater respect for the committee's decisions if they participated in the selection of its members.

Dr. Lawrence Kubie has seen this device used in a number of cases and is enthusiastic about its benefits. "In practice, such committees have done more than solve disputes. Their mere existence often protects the parents from reaching an impasse. As a result, such committees have had to be called into action only rarely. I have seen parents who had squabbled for years behave with restraint and generosity under the civilizing influence of the externalized conscience which the committee comes to represent." Kubie also advocates the appointment of an "adult ally," not usually a lawyer, in whom the child can confide.

The current custody process certainly has enough disadvantages to make any alternatives welcome, but the arbitration has its own weaknesses which also must be kept in mind. One is the problem of judicial enforcement and supervision of the committee's decisions. Although courts are usually willing to approve agreements parents make regarding custody of children — including, presumably, agreements to abide by an arbitrator's impartial decisions — they like to keep a hand in things. To the extent the court retains jurisdiction over the children, the committee's authority will be correspondingly undercut; if the court reviews every decision it makes, the committee will be only a recommending body.

Moreover, the success of the arrangement depends in large part on the willingness of both parents to accept it at the outset. The husband and wife must have reached a point where they are able to rise above their emotional differences and see that there are no simple right or wrong answers about raising their children. If the committee rules against them in a particular dispute, they must be able to accept the result without resentment. Ironically, the people who are mature enough to be well suited for the arbitration approach are probably those who least need to resort to it.

The most important question, Dr. Kubie's observations notwithstanding, is whether arbitration would deter disputes or encourage them. Its chief advantage — its ease of access — might mean that people would turn to it more than they do the courts; this might not always be for the better. Similarly, the effects of such a process on children are not fully apparent. Being examined by a committee of a half dozen people could be much more troubling for a child than being interviewed by one court investigator. Finally, it could be difficult to find enough good people to serve on such committees; the work would be demanding, sometimes in time and always in emotional energy. The sort of person who is best suited to serve may be overextended with other obligations. Although the arbitration method has been used for a number of years, it has not been thoroughly studied, so no one can be sure of its ultimate promise. Even if it does not prove to be a universal solution, it may be a desirable alternative for some families.

There are other ways of changing the manner in which we deal with custody problems. Although Judge Campbell's proposal — that some couples with children be barred from divorcing — is unrealistic, some kind of dual divorce procedure may be an appropriate way of reflecting the fact that society's interest is much greater in marriages with children than those with none. Childless couples might be permitted to divorce simply by registering their intent with an administrative bureau; in effect they would decline to renew their marriage license. Couples with minor children, however, should go through a more extensive process. The presence of children should not be used as a reason for denying divorce, but it is justification for more careful scrutiny on the part of the court to ensure that the interests of everybody involved, especially the children, have been protected. Arbitrary roadblocks cannot save dead marriages, but parents should be required to wait longer to receive a divorce than nonparents. The added time should not be so great as to be a hardship, yet it should be long enough to see if things can cool off. Freeing the courts from having to hear divorces of childless couples (unless there were a property dispute), would allow them to devote more time to those involving children. Similarly, if the state offers marriage counseling and other such resources, they should be directed to where they can produce the most good.

As a matter of practice, some judges already apply a dual standard for divorce, granting divorces routinely where there are no children, while giving more searching attention to the rest; but such a distinction should be drawn explicitly by statute, rather than be left to individual judges. Moreover, the specific creation of two kinds of divorce would also indirectly create two kinds of marriage; and this conceivably might cause people to consider more carefully the added responsibilities, moral and legal, of parenthood before having children.

Watson and others believe that if courts are to come to more intelligent decisions in custody cases, they must take better advantage of the skills and insights of social scientists. In order to determine what would be in the "psychological best interest" of the children, he proposes that examination of both parents and the children by clinical psychiatrists or other behavioral experts should be a prerequisite for any divorce involving children or subsequent custody action. The results of the examination would be turned over to the court. The New York law contemplates this kind of evaluation, but does not compel it. According to Watson, the procedure there is not used as often as it should be. "This suggests that if we wish to implement fully the psychological best interest of the child standard, it must be possible to force all parties to participate, or permit the court to draw negative inferences from their refusal. Unwillingness to participate in the examination should be prima facie evidence that the party does not have the child's best interest as a goal."

Watson's suggestion tests how seriously we are committed to discovering the best interests of the children. Will we tolerate unlimited invasions into a parent's privacy in attempts to protect the children? The proposal also challenges our faith in the social sciences. Lawyers and judges have traditionally been skeptical and, in some cases, hostile to any intrusion into their domain by social scientists. In recent years, however, there have been a number of members of the legal profession who have urged with all the zeal of the newly converted greater reliance on psychological and sociological evidence. As the *Painter* court's deference to the psychologist's testimony illustrates, this kind of evidence can be badly misused. Judges, like the rest of us, tend to avoid hard decisions, so there is a natural temptation on their part to accept the opinions of "experts," particularly if passing the buck can be disguised as deferring to the impartial truth of science. Until lawyers and judges are more sophisticated in their use of results of psychological examination, it should not be built into the system, lest it be given more weight than it deserves.

Regardless of what reforms are made in the substantive and procedural rules governing custody questions, one dilemma is likely to remain — the question of whether the court's decision ought to be final. Traditionally it has not been. Courts have been free to take custody away from one parent and give it to the other if there have been "changed circumstances" since the initial decree. The interpretation of changed circumstances varies somewhat from judge to judge, but many cases have held that the mere change in a child's age is sufficient to justify a court's reversing its original decision. Children inevitably grow older and other circumstances are bound to change, and this makes all custody decisions in effect temporary.

On one hand, it is easy to see the need for continuing judicial control over custody. If the parent with the children were to take on an extra job or were to become seriously ill, then he or she might not be able to give the children adequate care; in such instances it would be necessary to alter the custody arrangement. But this lack of finality has definite costs. Watson has stated, "When a child is kept suspended, never quite knowing what will happen to him next, he must likewise suspend the shaping of his personality. This is a devastating result and probably represents one of the greatest risks which current procedures pose for children."

This uncertainty also hurts the parents. The person who was not given custody will be tempted to scheme how to get it, instead of making the best of the situation. The parent with the children may feel that he or she is constantly on probation. These tensions will in turn strain their relationship with each other and the children. In many cases a final decision, even an arbitrary one, is preferable to leaving the matter open. Obviously a child's need for stability should not be blindly used to justify keeping it in a situation that threatens serious physical or emotional harm, but the court's power to review custody should be limited to extreme cases.

The primary danger is not possible meddling on the part of judges, but disgruntled parents' using the judicial process to harass their former spouses. The Uniform Marriage and Divorce Act requires a person to wait two years after filing a petition to modify a custody decree before bringing another one; the court can intervene, however, in emergency situations. Even without this sort of statutory direction, some state courts have acknowledged the importance of stability by refusing to modify a decree in spite of evidence that a change in custody might somewhat improve the child's environment. The more confidence that can be placed in the wisdom of the initial custody order, the less we need allow for later modification.

One state, acting alone, cannot completely solve the problem of uncertainty. As long as there is a chance that a court in another state will decide the case differently, there will be an inducement for a parent who loses custody to kidnap his or her own child in order to get the custody question retried. The Constitution requires that one state give "Full Faith and Credit" to the decisions of courts of other states, but this provision is often circumvented on the ground that changed circumstances justify a modification of the decree; that the child and one parent have moved to another state is sometimes regarded as sufficient change to warrant a complete review of the case. Homer Clark believes that the interstate rivalry among family courts is an unfortunate product of local chauvinism. "There is an impression current among many judges that divorce law is wholly local in nature; this attitude leads to the development of prejudice, provincialism, and the sort of scorn for judgments of other courts which is such a repulsive feature of custody litigation. Any practicing lawyer has experienced the practice of 'home-towning,' where the applicant for custody living in the state or district of the forum is preferred over the 'foreigner' from some other state."

The Commissioners on Uniform State Laws adopted the Uniform Child Custody Jurisdiction Act in 1968, and the A.B.A. quickly endorsed it. The statute, if it were enacted by all the states, would alleviate the dual problem of child snatching and judicial provincialism. In essence, the act allows a second state only to enforce the custody order of the first state that decided the matter; it is not permitted to modify it. The variation in all aspects of family law from state to state causes confusion and often injustice, but the need for uniformity is greatest in custody cases.

In summary, even though no custody process guarantees a happy solution to every case, a number of important improvements could be made in our present system. Too often in the past the custody process has been infected with fault notions; denial of custody has been arbitrarily used to punish certain kinds of marital misconduct. Although some aspects of marital behavior are relevant to the relationship between child and parent, it is time to abandon the overly moralistic approach and adopt one which gives the welfare of the children the greatest weight. In short, we need no-fault custody.

Any meaningful inquiry into the best interests of the children requires that judges and lawyers be experienced in family matters and at least familiar with the tools of other disciplines. As Foster has stated, "With reference to the policy of safeguarding the interests of the children of divorce, probably the most practical device is a mandatory requirement that there be independent counsel to represent the interests of the children. It is urgent that there be such protection where divorce is virtually automatic." So long as custody problems are handled by the courts, some sort of representation is necessary, whether by a lawyer or some other professional. The laws should also be revised to reflect the difference between marriages with children and those with none; family services should be concentrated on the former. Nonjudicial methods of resolving custody disputes should also be explored.

After committing ourselves to serving the best interests of the children of divorce and creating effective means to investigate the child's situation, we are left with the ticklish task of defining by what values the best interests of children are to be judged. Is it better for a young girl to remain with her mother who has not remarried, or should she go with her father who has? How much weight should be given to the child's expressed desires? By developing some sort of uniform conception of what is good for children, will we impose homogenized community standards on the children of divorce — should the courts deny custody to a parent who has unusual ideas about child-rearing? Or will we give judges great latitude to decide what is best in each situation, thereby risking that some will abuse this discretion? Such questions go to the heart of our most fundamental beliefs about the family and society's power to regulate it.

Innovation in custody laws and procedure has been slow in part because attitudes about parental roles have not changed until recently. That courts have mechanically awarded custody to women reflects a faith that their place is at home as mothers, while men should be working outside as breadwinners. The women's movement notwithstanding, a mother who does not want custody of her children, and a father who does, both have to cope with a society that will regard them as misfits. There is now more talk about granting custody to men, but no actual increase is apparent.

Ironically it is concern for the welfare of children that often sparks interest in improving our family laws, yet, after the dust of reform has settled, relatively little has been done for them. The California legislature made sweeping changes in its divorce law by eliminating the fault grounds and restructuring property rights; but, after much debate, it left the custody laws virtually unchanged. The Uniform Marriage and Divorce Act, which has been adopted by several states, wisely limits evidence of marital fault in questions of custody but does not provide for adequate investigation of the child's interest. Like other hard questions, the problem of determining sensible rules for child custody cases has been put off for another day. Undoubtedly it is impossible to satisfy everybody or to accommodate every consideration. The child's best interests may be contrary to the parents' right to raise the child as he or she sees fit. A child's need for stability must be balanced against the need for flexibility as circumstances change.

Because the controversy about child custody strikes so many emotional chords, the issue is usually tabled when family laws are revised. Compromise seems to lead back to the status quo, not out of any affection for the present system, but out of a feeling that reform of divorce laws should not be jeopardized by disagreement about what should be done about custody. As a result, the children of divorce have not been protected. The danger is that after a divorce reform bill is enacted, there may be a sense that the job is done, when actually one of the most important issues is still unresolved.

# Chapter Six

# Conciliation

The most common objection to no-fault divorce is the claim that it will encourage more divorce. We are warned that the divorce rate is already too high and that if people are allowed to end their marriages more or less at will, the rate will climb even higher. We are told that "easy" divorce breeds hasty divorce — people will end their marriages on impulse, rather than after careful thought. With our families crumbling, our morals threatened, and our tax bills going up because of welfare payments for broken homes, how can we think about making divorce any easier?

Such arguments have put reformers on the defensive. The benefits of divorce reform — less perjury and hostility — may seem amorphous while the costs appear very real. David Seidelson, who teaches at George Washington National Law Center, has observed that in order to make revision of the divorce laws politically palatable "some amulet must be displayed to the legislature, which it, in turn, can hold up to the public, to overcome the fear of increasing numbers of divorces and their consequences. What more politic manner of accomplishing this than a statutory scheme of marriage counseling aimed at preserving those marriages threatened with divorce but which may be salvaged? So systematic marriage investigation and counseling may become part of the price required for sensible divorce laws."

Court-connected marriage counseling is a price that many reformers have been willing to pay. In New York during the mid-sixties the hierarchy of the Catholic Church was strongly opposed to changing the existing law that granted divorce only for adultery; it was particularly opposed to letting people get a divorce simply after living apart for two years. It finally agreed to moderate its opposition in return for a guarantee that a provision would be written into the new law which would require every couple who wished to divorce to attend at least one conciliation conference. The original bill proposed by the legislative leadership had called for conciliation on a voluntary basis, but the Church had enough political power to force a clause which ostensibly made it mandatory for everyone.

Philip Shaeffer, a lawyer who was one of the drafters of the original bill, has said that the conciliation provisions in the bill ultimately enacted were considered by many as a "joke," a mere "sop" to appease religious leaders. One state senator said that a majority of his colleagues did not vote for compulsory conciliation out of any enthusiasm for the concept, but because they felt it was necessary to get the entire divorce reform package accepted. Even after the conciliation provision was enacted, support for it has been at best lukewarm. During the 1971–72 legislative session the New York Assembly voted to abolish the conciliation bureaus, but the Senate rescued them by a vote of thirty-one to twenty-four. In 1973 both houses voted overwhelmingly to kill the program; as of this writing, Catholics and others who supported conciliation were imploring Governor Nelson Rockefeller to use his veto to save it.

The Family Law Section of the A.B.A. has endorsed the principle of no-fault divorce, but it has steadfastly refused to approve the Uniform Marriage and Divorce Act, in part because the act makes no provision for conciliation. Judge Ralph Podell, a former chairman of the section, has said that he will go along with a no-fault approach only if there is some built-in check against hasty divorce. "There has to be some waiting or cooling-off period, and there has to be some kind of mandatory conciliation, that is, a mandatory inquiry whether there is a possibility of saving the marriage." The draftsmen of the Uniform Act apparently were split on the utility of conciliation and resolved their differences simply by avoiding the issue.

There are some good arguments that the courts ought to get

145125

EMORY & HENRY LIBRARY

into the business of marriage counseling. If society is truly interested in preserving marriages, then perhaps courts ought to do more than sit passively in marital disputes; instead of just deciding whether or not there should be a divorce, judges or someone else on the court staff might help the couple try to solve their underlying problems. A court-connected counseling service could perform both a real and a symbolic function, by directly helping as many people as it could and by demonstrating to others that there is a larger social interest in preserving marriages. Similarly, because many people who are in marital trouble end up in court, it may be an appropriate clearinghouse for information about other community services little known by the public. Even if a court program is unable to offer long-term counseling, it could direct people who want such assistance to an appropriate agency.

Judge Podell believes the best argument for requiring people to go through a conciliation program is that it gives them time to stop and think. When he practiced law, he saw many cases in which people had rushed headlong into divorce only to regret it later. "Once I had four cases in a row in which the man or the woman wanted a divorce so he or she could go back and marry a former spouse. I mention this to other lawyers and they laugh and say they've seen the same thing. It's just like October when the new cars come out. My tongue is hanging out to here, but after a week with the new car, I want my money and the old car back. We all need a little while to think."

Other judges who handle family matters agree that the delay imposed by a conciliation process has its own advantages. Arizona Judge Laurens Handerson has stated, "Time cures may ills and in these circumstances allows the spouses opportunity to reflect on their situation in light of the counseling before they come to a conclusion about reconciliation or divorce." Judge Paul Alexander of Ohio is another supporter of mandatory conciliation. He points to the fact that roughly thirty percent of all petitions for divorce brought in this country are eventually dropped before any final action is taken and suggests that many of the remaining seventy percent involve people who act too hastily. He believes that counseling can even help people who do not realize they need it. "Not everybody who appears to be demanding a divorce really wants one. You can't judge by how loudly they yell. Of those who think they want divorces, a great many would be better satisfied with some other form of relief. The overt acts, the superficial symptoms, mostly fall into stereotyped patterns; the underlying problems, the causal factors, vary considerably." Judge Alexander endorses the idea of no-fault divorce, but, as he conceives it, it would not be divorce for the asking. By means of a conciliation process, the state would inquire deeply into the condition of the marriage, not simply take the parties' word that it had broken down.

There are many cases, of course, in which reconciliation is impossible. If a person insists on divorce, he or she will not be swayed no matter how long or intensive the conciliation process. Yet counseling need not be useless in such cases. It can help such people resolve some of the important collateral issues, such as support, custody, and visitation. Divorce counseling may be just as important as marriage counseling, for a divorced couple must learn to adapt to the new roles and obligations they are about to assume. Although a counselor may not be able to save a given marriage, he may be able to make life easier for the couple and their children.

On the other hand, there are persuasive arguments against making marriage counseling a mandatory requirement for getting a divorce. If time is truly the best healer of marital wounds, then the simplest and cheapest way to make people look before they leap into divorce is to require a reasonable waiting period to pass after a petition is filed before the case will be heard. Paul Conway, who teaches at Georgetown University Law Center, believes, however, that if nothing is done to bring people together during the waiting period, time can have an unfavorable effect. "Instead of 'cooling-off,' many couples 'stew,' thus tending to intensify and reinforce what has been called 'conjugal paranoia.' " Yet this does not mean that any counseling program will suffice. Robert Coulson, an attorney with the American Arbitration Association, says that some of the conciliation services currently provided by courts "do little more than increase the cost and delay of final resolution, subjecting the parties to a long drawn-out series of interrogations by well-meaning social workers, court aides, and other appointees."

If a state is willing to spend a certain amount on saving marriages, it makes sense to funnel the money to those couples it would be most likely to help. Counseling is more successful if it can be undertaken before a marriage has deteriorated to the point where a divorce action has been started in the courts. Public funds may be better spent on preventing marital breakdown than on trying to rescue marriages which have already fallen apart. As for using the courts as clearinghouses, there are cheaper and more effective ways, such as advertising, to let people know of the availability of counseling resources. If people do not know of such help, they should be informed long before they have gone to court.

That legislatures are nevertheless more willing to fund marriage counseling for people about to divorce than other types of family service programs may be an example of what Thomas Schelling of Harvard University calls the El Capitan Principle. If a man gets stuck while making a foolhardy attempt to climb El Capitan bare-handed, we will send in as many rescue teams and helicopters as are necessary to save his life regardless of the risk. Yet if the same effort and expense were expended elsewhere — say, for prenatal care — it is possible that many more lives could be saved. Yet the man on the cliff has a name and the taut faces of his family appear on the television news each night until he is rescued. The identity of the babies who might be saved is unknown. So it is with marriage. We seem more inclined to try to rescue marriages perched on the precipice of divorce than to exert the same amount of effort more effectively to prevent many others from ending up there.

The strongest argument against requiring conciliation is that it threatens an undesirable — and conceivably unconstitutional — invasion of privacy. Society has a valid interest in attempting to preserve families, but an individual's right to refuse to reveal the intimacies of his or her marriage should be even greater. Henry Foster discounts this objection, maintaining that "the system does not force a party to stretch out on the psychiatric couch, to relate the story of his Oedipus complex, to submit to a lobotomy, or to endure brainwashing." He believes that no-fault divorce should not be adopted unless there is also some kind of service that verifies that the marriage is dead. "I don't recommend an inquest or an autopsy, just some kind of brake where somebody says,

'Whoa, wait a minute, are you sure you want a divorce?' I'm talking about screening not therapy. I've never suggested anything that would invade privacy."

Seidelson, a former student of Foster's, disagrees, contending that any meaningful screening process must necessarily involve inquiries into private matters. "If it does not, it is difficult to imagine how the interviewer can make an intelligent appraisal of the feasibility of 'further counseling sessions.'" Although Foster is an enthusiastic advocate of counseling programs, even he has some reservations. "It must be conceded, however, that from a psychological viewpoint the court counselor may be an authoritarian figure who influences the party into a course of action that otherwise might be rejected." Seidelson believes that this coercive factor is present even if the program is supposedly voluntary. In a pilot program in Maine ninety-seven percent of the people seeking divorce "volunteered" for counseling after they received a letter urging them to do so from the judge who would ultimately hear their cases. Although the judge's intentions were probably well-meaning, his letter had the effect of making the program compulsory, thus raising the same problem of invasion of privacy.

The propriety of court-sponsored conciliation programs, particularly the question of whether they should be mandatory, has been argued with some passion in the legal journals. It is difficult in the abstract to weigh the benefits of reaching out to all couples who bring marriage problems to court against the cost in terms of possibly invading some people's privacy. Similarly, there is dispute as to just how much good marriage counseling can do when it is conducted in the eleventh hour. Now that a number of states have operated different sorts of conciliation programs for some time, it seems more fruitful to see where they have succeeded and where they have failed.

As mentioned earlier, the conciliation program in New York has been on shaky footing politically since its creation in 1966. Whether or not Governor Rockefeller chooses to save it, its history illuminates both the difficulties encountered in trying to implement court-connected counseling and, equally important, the fact that such programs are often evaluated by erroneous standards. Before 1966 there had been some relatively small counseling projects in New York state, but they had involved only a few courts.

The new law established conciliation bureaus in each of the state's eleven judicial districts. Certain judges were designated to supervise the program, but their function has been largely titular; most of the responsibility and power has rested with the conciliation commissioner for each district. The qualifications for the position are not stringent — one must have been a member of the New York bar for at least five years, but special training or experience in counseling and family problems is not required. The job now pays thirty-four thousand dollars a year, which has made it an attractive sinecure for some former legislators and judges who failed to be reelected. One New York lawyer says of the commissioners, "They're nice enough guys, but a lot of them are political hacks."

Anyone who has begun a suit for divorce must notify the conciliation bureau. The law provides that "All parties shall be required to attend at least one conciliation conference, or may upon good cause shown and in the discretion of the commissioner, secure a certificate of no necessity for a conference and conciliation procedures shall be at an end." After this initial conference, which was apparently intended to be diagnostic, the commissioner may refer the parties to a counselor, who after a number of sessions may in turn request a second and presumably more exhaustive hearing before the commissioner. And after that hearing, the commissioner may request the court to order the couple to try to reconcile for up to sixty days.

On first reading, the new law may seem to require everyone who wants a divorce first to run through a lengthy gauntlet of commissioners and counselors, but in practice this has not been the case. A study made by the New York legislature's auditing arm reported that almost eighty percent of the people who file for divorce never see the commissioner for a single interview, let alone meet with a marriage counselor; the bureaus simply cannot handle the great numbers of people they are supposed to see. In 1972 there were over forty thousand notices of commencement of divorce, separation, or annulment, and that figure has been increasing steadily. Yet for the entire state of New York, there are only twelve commissioners, five deputy commissioners, and eight conciliation counselors. Because they are terribly understaffed, the commissioners routinely issue "certificates of no necessity for conciliation" in most cases.

The bureaus use a standard three-page questionnaire to select those couples who seem to be the most promising prospects for reconciliation. In addition to asking the parties' ages, the length of the marriage, and the number of children, the questionnaires ask people to note which problems exist in their marriage: finances, sex, in-laws, lack of social life, or raising of children. There is also a checklist of bad habits which can be attributed to one's spouse. The questionnaires confirm Seidelson's fear that even a superficial screening process can threaten people's privacy. There is something repulsive about asking people to record on an official state form that their sex life is bad.

Each commissioner has his own standards for determining which couples he should see personally and which should receive a waiver from participating. Some commissioners interview a couple only if one of them answered "yes" to the question, "Do you desire conciliation?" Others look to the length of time the couple has been separated — the longer the separation, the less likely they feel are the chances of getting the couple back together. Still others try to interview all couples who have minor children, in the belief that these marriages are the most important to save. The questionnaires are not intended to be scientific. Their interpretation depends in large part on who reads them, so a couple who must see the commissioner in one district might be "waived through" in another. As the policies of particular commissioners have become better known, people have learned to work around them. The legislative audit reported, "Most lawyers are quick to emphasize that they do not attempt to influence their clients' answers to the questionnaire; several indicated however that some members of the profession have their clients fill out the questionnaire in such a way that further conciliation is avoided. The extent of such practice is difficult to assess."

The twenty percent who are selected to attend a conference with the commissioner usually see him for less than an hour. Only a fraction of this group, ten to twenty-five percent, is referred for further counseling; the majority are allowed to proceed with their divorce if they wish. That so few are involved in actual marriage counseling — something less than five percent of all who file for divorce — reflects both the limited counseling resources and the fact that frequently one spouse resists any attempts at reconciliation. Although the commissioners have the power to refer people to outside counseling agencies, they seldom do, primarily because of the cost, which must be borne by either the individual or the state.

On its face, the New York law seems to require compulsory counseling, but only relatively few divorcing couples personally participate in the conciliation process and even they are not involved as deeply as the law seems to contemplate. There have been virtually no follow-up hearings before the commissioners, and no judge has ever invoked his power to order the parties to reconcile. If, after counseling, people still do not want to kiss and make up, they cannot be forced to, and most judges fear that compelling people to live together against their wills might lead to physical violence.

The New York conciliation program has suffered from two fundamental problems. One that has already been discussed is staff; there are not nearly enough qualified people to handle the workload. The program's lack of direction is an even greater weakness. Because it is the product of political compromise, the program has no solid constituency to make sure that it is functioning as was intended. In fact, its purposes have never been made very clear. This difficulty has been compounded by the Balkanized organization of the bureaus; how the program operates depends largely on the way the particular commissioner in charge interprets the mandate of the statute.

Not surprisingly, the conciliation program has come under continuing criticism. The legislative audit released in 1971 painted a bleak picture of its record. The investigators evaluated the bureaus in terms of the percentage of reconciliations relative to the total number of cases processed, that is, the number of matrimonial cases which were commenced in the state, and calculated the program's rate of success to be a dismal five percent. They reported that "Statistics indicate that the program is experiencing only marginal success in accomplishing the purposes of the legislation." The audit concluded that on the average it was costing taxpayers over four hundred dollars for each reconciliation that was achieved.

The investigation provided fuel for the argument that the reconciliation bureaus ought to be scrapped altogether, but the five percent rate that was emphasized was not a true measure of the program's effectiveness. Comparing the number of reconciliations to the total divorce cases filed is an unfair standard in that the conciliation bureaus did not have the resources to see nearly that many people. A somewhat fairer test might be the percentage of reconciliations for those people who actually conferred with a commissioner. According to the audit, this rate varied markedly from district to district; but the average for the entire state was eleven percent, still low, but a clear improvement over five. This figure is all the more respectable considering that most of the people who appeared before the commissioner did not participate in further counseling.

A more serious problem in trying to evaluate statistically the success of any conciliation program is distinguishing cause and effect. The New York Academy of Matrimonial Lawyers surveyed its members and reported many felt most of the reconciliations after conferences with a commissioner would have happened in any event. The bureaus should not be given full credit for every reconciliation they oversee. On the other hand, the mere existence of a conciliation program may have a beneficial effect on people who never participate in it. If people considering divorce, but have not yet filed for it, know they might have to go through a reconciliation process, they may have an incentive to try to work things out on their own. The argument for putting police road-blocks out on New Year's Eve is not just to catch drunken drivers, but to keep people from drinking if they plan to drive. The road-block of conciliation may be an inducement for some to resolve their problems privately. Those who succeed will never be counted in a legislative audit, yet they will have benefited from the existence of the program. Moreover, those who are unable to solve their differences on their own will obviously be harder cases for the counselors to handle. Because it is impossible to know precisely which reconciliations can be attributed to the program and which cannot, any percentage rating should be viewed suspiciously whether it be high or low.

According to Dorothy Maddi, who conducted an extensive study of conciliation programs under a grant from the A.B.A., "You can make reconciliation rates say anything you want them to, depending on what you base them. Unless everyone is seen in an effective system, you don't have any real basis for measurement, and even then a substantial number of reconciliations would probably occur without the program. But the New York audit made the record of the bureaus seem much worse than it really was."

Although it is often overlooked, the conciliation bureaus perform a valuable service when they help a divorcing couple reach agreement on financial and custodial matters. Jon McLaughlin interviewed a number of New York attorneys and found that "there is a widespread belief that conciliation services to help reach agreements on collateral issues are of great value to lawyers with relatively little experience in matrimonial litigation; however, such services are nuisances to experts. . . ." That experts discount the utility of conciliation may betray their jealousy at apparent intrusion into their specialty. Such an attitude ignores the fact that the way in which the agreement was reached may be just as important as its particular terms. That people have come to an understanding on their own, perhaps with a little coaxing from a counselor, may make it more likely that they will live up to it in the future than if the agreement were simply hammered out by their lawyers.

Much could be done to improve the New York conciliation program, especially increasing its manpower, raising its professional standards, and developing more uniform goals and methods. Undoubtedly it has fallen far short of its potential. But to criticize it for having only a five percent rate of reconciliations is to judge it by an unreasonable standard and to overlook the less tangible benefits of conciliation that do not lend themselves easily to quantification. Considering the savings in court time, lawyers' fees, and possible welfare payments, the elimination of the program by the legislature may be a case of being penny wise and pound foolish.

California's counties have had the option of creating conciliation courts for thirty-five years. Only a quarter of the state's fifty-six counties have done so, but those that have include major cities like Los Angeles, San Francisco, and San Diego. Unlike the New York law, the California statute makes it explicit that any counseling is voluntary, not compulsory. Those who file for divorce are

told of the conciliation courts, but they are not forced to participate. Moreover, the conciliation process is open to people whether
or not they have filed for divorce. As in New York, however, each
conciliation court has its own local focus. In Contra Costa County
there is long-term counseling, while in Los Angeles it is mostly
short term. Shasta County emphasizes public education, and San
Diego County has the reputation of being "particularly innovative."

Because each county has developed its own goals and methods,
it is hard to compare the success of one program against that of
another. Lewis Ohleyer, the Domestic Relations Commissioner in
San Francisco, believes that the percentages of marriages saved is
a misleading statistic. "For one thing we get involved in cases at
different points in time. Obviously there is a better chance of
reconciliation before a couple has started divorce proceedings
than if we don't get to see them until they have taken the step of
filing the necessary papers. Second, we try to do some good for
everyone we see. If people reconcile, so much the better, but even
if they don't, we feel we've done some positive good if we can
help them part on more friendly terms."

The goal of the counselors in Los Angeles is to get the parties
to sign a reconciliation agreement acknowledging each other's
rights and setting out rules for dealing with future marital problems. The final document often runs twenty-five pages or longer.
Some of the standard provisions are quite specific: "Each party
agrees not to give the other the 'silent treatment' by refusing to
engage in normal conversation for extended periods of time."
Other clauses read like Dear Abby's observations on marriage
without the wisecracks: "The importance of love-making in the
first stages of intercourse must not be ignored."

Most lawyers snicker at these agreements, because they are
binding only so long as both parties are willing to observe them.
A judge does approve each agreement, thus giving the court the
power to order compliance, but the subject matter of the contract
is such that compulsion is impossible; people who breach the
agreement are never found to be in contempt of court. Ohleyer
declines to use such a device in his office, noting, "You'd have
to be pretty naïve to sign it." Nevertheless, most people who are
brought back together in the Los Angeles conciliation court do
consummate their reconciliation by executing the agreement. It is

not binding, but it does serve several important functions. First, it forces the husband and wife to address specific problems. Each agreement includes a budget which the couple has worked out; for many, it is the first time they have sat down together to figure out money problems. Also, because the clauses are fairly standard (they are modified to fit individual situations), they carry the implicit message that many of the difficulties the parties face are not peculiar to them but are natural to any two people trying to live under one roof. When they accept the standard clauses as part of their personal agreement, the parties can feel they are conforming to larger social norms, not simply private compromises. In other words, by signing the agreement, they are doing the "right thing."

Similar reconciliation agreements are used in Arizona. As Judge Laurens Henderson of Phoenix has commented, "One may ask whether this agreement is enforced. The answer is, quite frankly, no. The value of the contract is its psychological effect deriving from the fact the husband and wife have solemnly and voluntarily made mutual promises to each other in a law court."

The most important advantage of having people sign a formal reconciliation agreement is the one most frequently overlooked, even by marriage counselors. The agreement looks official. It carries the name of the county court on the first page, the signature of the conciliation counselor (and sometimes the judge) on the last, and there are numerous pages of provisions in between. Because of its very weight, both real and symbolic, it provides a tangible alternative to getting a divorce. A person who feels he or she has been driven to the point of desperation, who has said so publicly by seeking a divorce, can have trouble returning to the marriage without looking as if he or she backed down. A formal, written agreement offers an out, a way of saving face, not just in respect to others, but also to oneself. Instead of feeling that one has compromised oneself by deciding to go back to the same old unbearable marriage, a person can feel that in a sense he or she has remarried his or her spouse on new and better terms.

The percentage of people who participate in the Los Angeles program and are ultimately reconciled has been consistently high; in some years more than half the couples agreed to stay married. Follow-up studies show that most of them are still together several years later. The high rate is largely due to the fact the program is voluntary; by making the decision to take part, the people have already demonstrated that they have not closed all the doors behind them. If one or both of the spouses adamantly wants a divorce, it is unlikely they will be involved in the program. This self-selection also means that relatively few people are reached; roughly ten percent of all those who petition for divorce go through the conciliation court. That people can get counseling before filing for divorce also improves the average.

The success of the Los Angeles project is not due solely to the fact that counselors can concentrate their efforts on couples who have the best chance of reconciling. Much of it is due to the high professional quality of the conciliation staff; counselors are required to have at least a master's degree in one of the social sciences as well as extensive practical experience. The use of conciliation agreements, as unsophisticated as they may seem, is certainly another positive factor. Finally, the Los Angeles conciliation court has the advantage of age; it has been in existence since 1939, so the program has a strong sense of pride and direction.

As the conciliation courts in other counties have somewhat different aims — some try to reach more people and others emphasize divorce counseling — the overall reconciliation rate for the California programs is lower, about twenty-eight percent, than that for Los Angeles alone. This does not mean that the Los Angeles program is any better; indeed, success should be measured in terms of how many people have been helped to clarify their goals, how much tension has been reduced, and the extent to which collateral issues have been resolved. Judged by this standard most of the California programs have worked quite well.

Because of this history of success, the Governor's Commission on the Family recommended, as part of its reform statute, making an initial interview in a conciliation court mandatory for all people who wished to divorce. According to Herma Kay, who fought hard for this provision, the interview was intended only to be diagnostic, not therapeutic. "The sole function of the mandatory initial interviews is to discover the current situation in order to help the parties see their own situation clearly and to make available to them such of the court's services as they may choose." Richard Dinkelspiel, the cochairman of the commission, saw an added reason for requiring an interview. "We wanted a screening process, not compulsory counseling, but some procedure so the courts at least could begin to gather a body of knowledge about what was really causing divorce."

Somewhat to the commission's surprise, the conciliation provision was strongly attacked during the legislative debate. The commission tried hard to characterize the procedure as being only "screening," but the opponents insisted on calling it "forced marriage counseling," a description that made the proposal seem both coercive and unrealistically expensive. It was contended that it would cost the counties one hundred million dollars a year to pay the salaries of the additional counselors that would supposedly be made necessary. Such projections bore no relation to reality, but they sufficiently tainted the proposal so that it was eventually cut from the family law reform package. As a result, conciliation is available only in those California counties which havé chosen to have it and even there it is still voluntary. Kay feels the defeat of the conciliation proposal was the biggest disappointment in the new law. She regretted it particularly because, since many of the present programs "limit their resources to marriage counseling in an attempt to produce reconciliations, one of the commission's most imaginative ideas — that of divorce counseling — is lost."

The statutes of a number of other states contemplate attempts at reconciliation, but in some, such as Vermont, the reconciliation provisions are rarely invoked. In others, however, they are an important part of the process. A 1960 Wisconsin law requires any person who wants a divorce in that state first to attend at least one conciliation conference; the defending spouse cannot stall a divorce by refusing to participate in conciliation, but he or she is encouraged to take part. All screening is done by personal interview rather than by questionnaire. There has been a serious commitment to finance the program; Milwaukee alone has eleven counselors, compared to eight for the entire state of New York. In the period 1956–59, when conciliation was only voluntary, thirty-nine percent of the divorce cases initiated were eventually dropped. Since conciliation has been made compulsory, this figure has increased by roughly six or nine percentage points. It would be incorrect to conclude that conciliation now saves almost half the marriages headed for divorce, however, because a fair share of the cases would have been dropped in any event. But it is interesting to see that the proportion of cases dropped did increase somewhat after participation became compulsory.

On balance, making counseling a part of the divorce process seems like a good idea. There are private and public agencies in every state which offer marriage counseling, but they do not reach enough people. A court gets to people when they are in trouble and thus is in a good position to give help if it is needed. No other institution can serve this function. Some lawyers oppose court-connected counseling systems on the ground that they can satisfactorily advise their clients and, if need be, send them to marriage counselors. There are many lawyers, however, who make no real effort to reconcile their clients' problems; some justify this by saying that it is not their role to play God with other people's lives. One attorney says, "If my client has hired me to get a divorce, I really don't think I can substitute my judgment for his; and if I do, the first thing he'll say is, 'Send me your bill and I'll go to someone who will do it,' because there's bound to be another lawyer who will take the case."

The lawyers who take the opposite position do not necessarily serve their clients any better — beware of the lawyer who describes himself as an "amateur psychologist." Often such people have inflated opinions of their talents as marital mediators. Bill Loud, whose divorce was documented in the television series *An American Family*, later laughed about the feeble efforts his lawyer made at reconciliation. "The lawyer starts out the blurb by saying, 'Well now, I'd like to keep this marriage together . . . isn't there any way that I can . . . wouldn't it be better if you just took a vacation with your wife?' Christ, I've been takin' her on a vacation every two months. So then — that's the first ploy, you see. The next ploy is, he says, 'I think your big problem is you're traveling too much.' And I said, 'I think you're right. I'm traveling too much, but if we're going to live in this way that we've accustomed ourselves, I got to travel that much.' " After having gone through the process, Loud dismissed divorce lawyers as a bunch of "fakealoos."

Lawyers who profess to be reconciliation-oriented report strikingly different rates of success; some say they can dissuade only one client in ten from divorce, while others claim they reconcile two out of three. The difference is not simply one of skill, but also the kind of practice the lawyer has. A specialist in divorce who receives referrals from other lawyers is likely to have a much poorer reconciliation average than a general practitioner, because the clients the specialist sees tend to be much farther down the road to divorce. In either case, as Paul Conway has noted, good intentions are not a substitute for professional training in marriage counseling. "Experience has demonstrated that the well-meaning attorney who relies solely on his own skills to reunite estranged parties seldom achieves lasting success."

Any lawyer who encourages his client to reconcile with his or her spouse faces an ethical conflict. While working with both parties (assuming he has the blessing of the other spouse's attorney), he must keep in mind that his efforts may fail. One day he may be counseling two people to compromise and work things out, and the next he may have to fight for the best possible divorce settlement for his client.

There is also a conflict of economic interest. What is best for the client and his family may not be best for the lawyer. Because of this, Judge Alexander has concluded, "It would be unduly optimistic to look to the bar to screen out the unwanted, unneccessary, and undesirable divorces." After serving on the bench for more than thirty years, he has little regard for most divorce lawyers. "For them divorce is their rent, their stenographer's salary, their baby's shoes, sometimes their solid gold Cadillac. The simplest uncontested case is generally worth a couple of hundred dollars; a case involving even a moderately well-to-do husband accused (not necessarily guilty) of infidelity is ordinarily worth a few thousand to the lawyers. How unrealistic to expect them to forgo anything like that for mere considerations of ethics or morals." Whether Judge Alexander's scornful description really applies to most divorce lawyers or to just a minority does not change his point. We cannot fully depend on all lawyers to steer their clients away from unnecessary divorce. Even if some lawyers will, others will not, either out of financial self-interest or out of ignorance of counseling techniques.

There are many lawyers who recognize their own limitations and try to send their clients to professional marriage counselors.

Good counseling, however, is not always available; investigations in a number of states have exposed many charlatans. Boston lawyer Brooks Potter notes another problem: "Private counseling is expensive, simply out of the reach of most people. It works for some, and that's fine, but the great majority can't afford it for any length of time." Not every community has public counseling services. As a result we must turn to the courts.

The increase in the percentage of reconciliations in Wisconsin after that state went from voluntary to compulsory conciliation proceedings indicates that there may be something gained by requiring everyone to participate. But there is something lost as well. To be effective, any diagnostic interview must delve into private matters. Although people ostensibly have the right not to answer questions, the atmosphere is often such that it is hard to say no. Even the three-page screening questionnaire used in New York asks people to declare for the record the source of their marital problems. On balance the small gain in making a program mandatory is not worth the cost in terms of the resulting invasion of privacy. There is nothing wrong with urging people to take advantage of the service so long as they know they will not be penalized for declining to do so. People must be absolutely sure the judge will not treat their divorce case differently if they have not gone through counseling.

Dorothy Maddi observes, "There used to be a heated debate whether counseling should be mandatory or voluntary, but people are coming to realize that compulsory counseling for everyone just isn't possible, particularly in populous areas — it's just too expensive to be politically feasible. Perhaps you can have mandatory screening, but the question then is whether it should be by questionnaire or personal interview. The method used makes a big difference in who is selected for counseling."

Even though compulsory marriage counseling is probably neither desirable nor possible, we should still try to reach those people who strongly want divorce and do not wish to be bothered with fruitless attempts at reconciliation. For them there should be a separate service to help them adapt to their new obligations; it should be termed "divorce counseling" so as not to scare off its potential clientele. Getting people past the counselor's door might lead a few people to reconsider their decision to divorce. Even for those who go ahead, as most can be expected to do, there should be important benefits, as Herma Kay has emphasized. "Paradoxically, divorce counseling can become one of the most effective forms of marriage counseling. Although it may be difficult to persuade two persons who are eager to marry that they should delay their plans to take a second look at their chances of success in the marriage, it should be relatively easy to demonstrate to two people whose marriage has just failed the value of attempting to gain the self-awareness to avoid another mistake. Although great care must be taken to avoid coercion, affording the opportunity for voluntary reexamination of past marriages seems to be a realistic and desirable way of expressing the state's interest in the stability of future marriages."

Marriage counseling is no cure-all, especially when it comes after one of the spouses has asked for divorce. Voluntary court conciliation program services may not actually change many people's minds, but in a significant number of cases they can provide a very useful face-saving device to allow people to back away from a hasty decision. In essence, it can help people do what they really want to but are afraid to do on their own. As a result it is probably unnecessary for a court to offer long-term counseling. If a couple needs it, they can be referred to an outside agency. The face-saving aspect of conciliation will work, however, only if the public respects the program. High professional standards will both contribute to its effectiveness and prevent it from looking like a political boondoogle.

When no-fault divorce is proposed, there is much talk about the enormous social interest in preserving marriages. Divorce supposedly costs the state money in courthouses, welfare payments, and juvenile delinquency. Yet it is ironic that when conciliation programs intended to save marriages are proposed, they are often trimmed or voted down because of their cost. Until now few legislatures have really put their money where their platitudes are. A careful study of all the benefits would show that it would be money well spent.

# Chapter Seven

# Divorce Yourself

Nathaniel Denman, the founder of Family Law Reform, Inc., in Massachusetts, does not like divorce lawyers. He claims they are biased against men, disloyal to their clients, and, in too many cases, incompetent. Exorbitant attorneys' fees are the final indignity. "When a lawyer asks for eight hundred dollars for an uncontested divorce, I think it is a swindle and a scandal. He's not charging on the time that he's going to put in, but on the fact that his client needs a divorce badly. If it's uncontested, it's going to take him ten minutes in court plus a few dollars to pay his secretary to fill out the forms."

Denman's mission is to put lawyers out of the divorce business. He urges many of the people who contact him to handle their own divorces, though he admits that under present laws this is not always easy. He complains that divorce laws have been kept deliberately "mystifying," so that people will be forced to turn to lawyers for help, when they should in fact be able to do it themselves. To him the solution is simple: eliminate the hocus-pocus from the law, and thus cut out the middle-man — the lawyer — from the divorce process. Denman supports no-fault divorce because he believes it will let more people be their own lawyers.

Denman is wrong, however, in both his facts and his conclusion. He exaggerates the cost and minimizes the work involved in divorce. Lawyers do not charge set fees. Until recently many bar associations did publish "minimum fee schedules," but at best they provided only a rough guide to charges. The use of the word minimum was somewhat misleading — perhaps intentionally so. Lawyers were not required to bill according to the schedule, but their clients were more apt to swallow a substantial fee if it could be rationalized as the minimum set by the bar. These fee schedules are now being withdrawn, as the result of accusations that they are really price-fixing arrangements in restraint of trade.

The schedules may have indicated the approximate cost of an average divorce case, but there has always been a great deal of variation up and down. Cases involving high fees make the news, while those with low fees do not. For example, Minneapolis newspapers gave front-page coverage to a bar association investigation of a lawyer who allegedly tried to charge a janitor, who earned one hundred dollars a week, seventy-five hundred dollars for a divorce. The attorney contended that complicated negotiations over property justified a bill of many thousands, but he ultimately settled for fifteen hundred dollars, because he was in his words "panic-stricken" by the "unfair publicity" the case had received in the media. Fees are often based on what the client can bear, and instances of gouging are not rare. Brooks Potter, who has practiced domestic law in Boston for four decades, says, "Some of our lawyers are outrageous on fees. I'm afraid there are a lot who are more interested in their fee than the welfare of their client." Often the fee is reasonable, but because it comes at a time when family finances are tight, it may seem unfair. Moreover, the custom of requiring the husband to pay the fees of both his own lawyer and his wife's undoubtedly makes the burden appear doubly harsh.

Because big fees are a mark of status within the profession, lawyers are reluctant about revealing what they charge. Nobody wants the reputation of running a cut-rate office. One California lawyer confided, "Those other bastards say they charge a thousand dollars, but I don't believe it. We do it for three-fifty or four hundred. If somebody comes in who can't pay that, we'll go down to one hundred fifty, which is probably our break-even point, what with the paper work, the marital settlement, and the hassling involved in getting people to read and sign it. I want people to understand it before they sign, so it takes a couple of meetings and a court appearance."

A lawyer who gets more than a couple of hundred dollars for a divorce is not necessarily robbing his client. Tim Savinar, a San Francisco attorney, says, "Even if both people want the divorce, they usually don't agree on all the details of property division or child support. I end up in the position of mediator. If I represent the wife, I often have to persuade her that she can't ask for the moon; and if I'm working for the husband, part of my job is to make him see that he has continuing obligations to his family. Negotiating with your own client can take a lot of time."

Even if the legal and financial issues are straightforward, the emotional aspects of divorce can be draining for the lawyer. According to Norman von Rosenvinge, a Boston attorney, "Divorce isn't just a matter of drawing up papers, getting witnesses in court, and going through the patter. It's a long, drawn-out process of finding out what is wrong and attempting to rectify it. Now if you do rectify it, it's pretty hard to send out more than a nominal bill, even though you've spent a lot of time on the case. And oddly enough, you haven't gained much in the way of good will. People are often ashamed of the whole thing, so that if they have legal problems in the future, they may be too embarrassed to bring them to you."

Von Rosenvinge also thinks that lawyers are often underpaid for those cases which do end in divorce. "How much is a call to your home at two in the morning worth? Your client calls to say that her husband has beaten her up or has threatened suicide or has run off with the children. You get used as a wailing wall, and you are really the only one available. If you have any kind of feeling for people, this kind of thing starts to gnaw at your guts. But clients are funny. They expect you always to be available and sympathetic, yet they balk at paying the bill that kind of personal service requires."

That divorce is regarded as an emotional, messy business keeps most lawyers out of family law. One Boston lawyer, who now specializes in criminal cases, gave up his divorce practice after a client's husband tried to shoot him. "Sandman" Williams burst into a Reno courtroom where his divorce was being heard and killed two lawyers. Most divorce lawyers have somewhat better luck, but many admit to ulcers, depression, or a hardening of the emotional arteries. At one time, von Rosenvinge had a fair amount of divorce work, but he now refers it to other lawyers on the ground that it is "a young man's game." The legal profession has its caste system, and those who handle divorce are stuck with the stigma of dealing with a slimy area of the law. Divorce is to the practice of law as proctology is to medicine. As mentioned in Chapter Six, Judge Paul Alexander of Toledo feels there may be a kind of reverse Darwinian selection — that is, a survival of the unfittest — that accounts for the greed and corruption he sees in divorce practice.

Family lawyers are understandably defensive about their lack of status, but whenever they try to improve their image by organizing support for some kind of reform, they are accused of acting solely out of self-interest. In failing to endorse specific no-fault legislation, the Family Law Section of the A.B.A. has been criticized as a self-serving organization, interested only in making sure there is enough work for its members. This accusation angers its recent chairman, Judge Ralph Podell. "We are accused of being the shadiest, you might say the sleeziest, outfits connected with the A.B.A. We don't come within the affluent categories like the corporation lawyers or tax specialists, but we have nothing to be ashamed of." Unfortunately much of the debate on no-fault divorce within the legal profession has deteriorated to an exchange of *ad hominem* attacks on motives rather than a discussion of the merits. Many family lawyers, defensive about their position to begin with, see the movement for no-fault divorce as the work of academics and social scientists out of touch with the realities of everyday practice. Judge Podell has said, "To me, those persons in the legal profession who really want no-fault are those who don't know how to handle a divorce case. They want to have the benefit of making money out of a divorce case without putting any effort into it."

There are many others, however, who see no-fault as a plot to get all lawyers out of divorce. Charles Mentrowski, Associate Dean of Marquette Law School, chided the members of the Family Law Section, "I really relish this no-fault business that you lawyers talk about. Behind it all, you can't see that it's really 'no-lawyer.' Whether it is no-fault insurance law or administrative probate or now no-fault divorce, you're all advocating your own demise. The reformers have done such a fine job, they've made themselves no longer necessary. Of course, I can talk this way because I don't rely on the practice of law for my income."

Such warnings are not falling on deaf ears. Lawyers are alert to every small sign that their practices may be threatened. In state after state, "do-it-yourself" divorce kits are being sold — perhaps illegally — for a hundred dollars or less. This has made lawyers jittery and though the movement for no-fault divorce got started quietly, the word is now out among lawyers that it is another scheme to put them out of business. Many who feel they have been burned by no-fault automobile insurance plans are determined not to let the same thing happen to them with divorce. Some are frank enough to admit that they do not want to lose a healthy part of their income, but most couch their objections in terms of concern for the public. After hearing Mentrowski speak, an Indiana lawyer blurted out, "I've read everything there is about no-fault divorce, I've talked to lawyers in states which have adopted it, and I'm convinced it is the biggest hoax imaginable. By putting in no-fault divorce, you're letting people get the forms and handle their own cases. You're cheating people of the professional representation, the professional advice that a good family lawyer can provide."

This impression, that no-fault divorce means no-lawyer divorce, is shared by many people like Nathaniel Denman who support reform and by others who oppose it. Ironically, both factions are wrong. For better or worse, where no-fault divorce has been adopted, it has helped lawyers, not hurt them. Lawrence Stottert, the chairman of the Family Law Section of the California Bar Association, maintains, "There is no one I know of who practices family law to any extent who has been hurt by the passage of the new law. Even with the growing legal assistance programs, which have carved a lot of the marginal cases out of some lawyers' practices, there have been no complaints. All the arguments that no-fault divorce would adversely affect the monetary interests of lawyers have been proven to be absolutely untrue."

California's adoption of irreconcilable differences as the sole ground for divorce did greatly simplify the legal procedures. Judge Byron Lindsley says, "Any intelligent person can fill out the simple forms himself." As noted in Chapter Two, the testimony in court for an uncontested divorce usually involves just saying "yes" to four or five questions which establish residency and the existence of irreconcilable differences. Because of the streamlined procedures, there has been an increase in the number of people who represent themselves in divorce court, yet the newspaper headlines proclaiming "Do-it-yourself Divorce Soars in California" are misleading. Rough estimates indicate that one in every twenty California divorces is brought without a lawyer, compared to less than one for every hundred previously. This might be characterized as a five hundred percent increase, but relative to the total number of divorces heard, it is still only a handful. Considering that the total number of divorces has risen by almost fifty percent over the same period, there is no need to take up collections for needy lawyers who have been put out of business. The overall increase in the number of divorces has greatly exceeded the growth in pro se cases, that is, cases in which people represent themselves.

Those people who do try to handle their own cases usually get little help from the California courts. Judge Walter Carpeneti of San Francisco says, "I'm in the minority. Most judges have taken the position they will be of no assistance to the litigants. People come up on the stand, and unless they know what questions to ask themselves and what documents to present, nothing happens. They're out of luck. A few judges, like myself, figure that if they have gone to all this trouble and it is really a simple dissolution, then it's all right for us to ask the questions, but I suppose that in a way we're playing the role of an attorney. And as lawyers become more aware of it, I expect they will object." According to Judge Carpeneti, more and more of his colleagues are taking a sink-or-swim attitude toward people who represent themselves. "They say it isn't their job to be attorneys too, and maybe they're right. If somebody wants to present his own case, then perhaps he should do it correctly." At first judges took a more tolerant view, but many soon tired of watching people do poor imitations of Perry Mason; as former lawyers themselves, some judges are hostile to amateurs trying to play their game.

It has not been the judges' general reluctance to assist litigants that has kept California divorce lawyers in business; rather it has been the nature of the real problems of divorce. Beverly Hills attorney Stuart Walzer has noted, "There is a common assumption that if the concept of fault were removed from divorce, the role of the lawyer would disappear. This is not true. The lawyer's services are needed in determining the nature and extent of the marital assets, their origin, and their present status. Often, once these facts have been determined, support can be set and the assets can be divided with a minimum of difficulty. The question of marital fault is only a minor element in some jurisdictions."

Richard Dinkelspiel, a San Francisco attorney who was at the forefront of the push for no-fault legislation, thinks most divorces still need a lawyer's attention. "Where there are children or complicated property problems, divorce cases have always been and will always be economically sound, both for the client and the lawyer. I've always questioned whether or not the lawyer who gets a hundred and fifty or two hundred dollars for an uncontested divorce really makes any money, when he gets through preparing the pleadings, serving the people, and going into court. That kind of case has always been marginal for a lawyer and remains so today. It's not a good, stable kind of practice. If people don't have much money, you're limited in what you can charge. Of course, people with money are going to have special tax and property problems, but they also have the wherewithal to pay for solutions."

What has been true in California has also been the case in other states: lawyers are prospering under no-fault. Yet oddly this fact has not registered elsewhere. People on both sides of the fence still cling to the belief that no-fault is synonymous with no-lawyer and this fallacy has dominated and distorted the debate on reform. It is as if cartographers were still arguing whether or not the world is square or rectangular.

Neil Chayet, chairman of the Family Law Section of the Massachusetts Bar Association, feels the term no-fault is an albatross around reformers' necks because of its association with automobile insurance plans. "It's all right to talk about 'marital breakdown' and 'living apart,' but the minute you say 'no-fault divorce' in front of our legislators, it's the kiss of death. Most of them are small town lawyers and they won't even talk about something that sounds like it might cost them money." This instinctive negative reaction is ironic, as it apparently is contrary to the legislators' personal interest; yet it does explain why so little has been learned from those states which have enacted no-fault divorce. Many lawyers blindly oppose anything described as "no-fault" and shut their ears to information which might change their minds.

Samuel Schoonmaker, chairman of the Connecticut Bar Association's Family Law Section, does not think he was cutting his own throat economically by lobbying for the no-fault legislation recently enacted in that state. "About fifty or seventy-five percent of my practice is domestic relations work. I don't think no-fault will have any adverse affect on this practice at all. But it will greatly improve the quality of family law. It will mean we won't have to engage in all the wheel-spinning we've done up till now. We have had to argue about who hit whom first or whether there was adultery, but that's all beside the point. The real contest involves custody of the children, visitation, division of assets, and support. Anybody who has been married knows that when there is a fight, it is rarely just one person's fault. It's hardly ever cut and dried in divorce, so it's like chasing your own tail when you are trying to find out who is at fault. It's a waste of the lawyer's time, it's a burden on the judiciary, and it costs the client money."

Schoonmaker's arguments are persuasive, but there was an influential segment of the Connecticut bar that chose not to listen. "There were some lawyers who felt no-fault would make an impact on the little cases, the cases where the husband earns one hundred dollars a week, and the wife works part time for fifty. There are single practitioners in rural areas who get a fee of several hundred dollars for divorcing such people and they are afraid that no-fault will dry up this business. They think a lot of these people will do it themselves. Even if this is true — and I'm not sure it is — I don't think it is a good reason for opposing reform that is socially necessary." Schoonmaker found lawyers, like most people, are not receptive to "social reform" if they think it is going to cost them money.

This kind of myopic rejection has bogged down the divorce reform movement in many states, but Judge Podell resents the suggestion that the same kind of imagined self-interest is behind the A.B.A.'s reluctance to endorse a specific no-fault bill. "Look at me. I'm a judge. I've got nothing to gain by keeping things the way they are. Any form of no-fault would mean a lot less work for me, but that would be a pretty poor reason for my supporting it."

Judge Podell has some doubts about no-fault divorce, but he says they stem from reasons other than protecting lawyers' business. "I don't care if people get their own divorces. And I'd feel that way if I were still practicing. You don't want that kind of client anyway. You can't make any money, and he's a headache to you. So I'm not worried about that. What concerns me is doing the right thing for society. If that means eroding a certain area of legal practice, so be it." He is careful to stress that the Family Law Section has endorsed the principle of no-fault divorce. It has simply rejected the specific formulation suggested by the Commissioners on Uniform State Laws. "Their bill is about thirty-five pages long, so it's not just a statement of 'irretrievable breakdown.' There are a number of serious points which have caused us to oppose this particular bill: the provision for division of property is poorly drafted, divorce can be granted too quickly, and there is no real provision for conciliation. These are important issues, but in the press it is interpreted that we are opposed to no-fault divorce. That isn't so."

It is hard to know whether to take seriously the Family Law Section's "endorsement in principle" of no-fault divorce. Perhaps it is an attempt by the section to have its cake and eat it too. It can pay lip service to the idea, thus getting reformers off its back to an extent, without really committing itself to its adoption. The press and lawyers throughout the country have interpreted the section's action as simple opposition to no-fault. John Williams, an officer of the Vermont Bar Association, says the legislature in his state declined to adopt the Uniform Marriage and Divorce Act largely because of the "hesitation" of the A.B.A. to endorse it. Although Vermont did add a liberal separation ground, it retained the traditional fault-oriented causes. Thus the fact that the A.B.A. appears to have been dragging its feet on divorce reform has made states somewhat cautious about adopting no-fault plans, particularly the Uniform Act.

In fairness, however, it is true that the Uniform Act is an extensive piece of legislation, and, even though many people approve of it generally, it is hard to build a coalition of people who support all its provisions. The Commissioners on Uniform State Laws first presented the act to the A.B.A. in 1970. The Family Law Section strongly disapproved it, and since that time representatives of the commissioners and the section have tried to fashion an acceptable compromise. Although the commissioners went along with substantial amendments, the section has continued to withhold its endorsement. In 1973 the section proposed a counterdraft which among other major changes eliminated irretrievable breakdown as a ground for divorce. It substituted a dual standard: either that there has been a year's separation preceding the action for the divorce or that "such serious marital misconduct has occurred which has so adversely affected the physical or mental health of the petitioning party to make it impossible for the parties to continue the marital relation and that reconciliation is improbable." The stark language of the second ground makes it clear that, when the section previously endorsed the principle of no-fault, it was not thoroughly committed to abolishing all vestiges of fault theory from divorce law. As of this writing, the impasse between the A.B.A. and the Commissioners on Uniform State Laws has not been resolved.

There are undoubtedly some lawyers who are trying for selfish reasons to use the bar associations to block reform efforts, but it is an oversimplification to make the Family Law Section of the A.B.A. the villain in the dispute about no-fault divorce. Judge Podell points out that family lawyers are damned if they oppose divorce reform and damned if they don't. "I appeared before the Wisconsin legislature to advocate some modernization of the law, and there was the accusation that the organized bar was supporting 'easier' divorce in order to make more money. Then, after the Family Law Section decided not to support the Uniform Marriage and Divorce Act, the papers said we were against it because we stood to make more money the way things are. We can't win. After that, I figured it was high time to get out of the practice and become a judge."

Many family lawyers oppose no-fault divorce, out of either genuine doubts about its social desirability or more commonly, an erroneous fear that it will cost them money. Reformers thus have had to take a low profile to avoid alarming the potential opposition. Louise Raggio, as chairman of the Family Law Section of the Texas Bar Association, was able to shepherd a no-fault provision through her state legislature as part of a much more extensive reform of Texas' family laws. "We went through very quietly. That was our strategy. We knew that the legislature wouldn't buy abolishing all the old grounds for divorce, so we simply proposed 'insupportability of the marriage' as an additional ground. As it has turned out, eighty-five percent of divorces are now brought under this no-fault ground; but when we proposed it, it didn't look so earth-shattering."

Now that it has been enacted, no-fault has the strong support of Texas lawyers. "There has been some increase in the number of divorces," says Mrs. Raggio, "so if anything, lawyers are making more money today." That she and her colleagues were able to get any reform through their conservative legislature is a tribute to their skill and persistence; still the net result is that the Texas law represents only half a loaf. The old fault grounds remain on the books and can be used by a spouse who wants to be vindictive. Then too, some Texas courts have tended to want more than a unilateral allegation of insupportability of the marriage. The required evidence can involve the same kind of emotional issues which breed hostility and division under the traditional fault system. Once a compromise between the old law and the new is reached, it can be difficult to push for further reform, even though the original opponents may have been won over; the reformers understandably lose steam, and inertia prevails. Given the political realities in many states, however, a compromise is better than nothing.

Whether reform of divorce laws is total, as in California, or partial, as in Texas, no-fault divorce has not hurt lawyers. Nathaniel Denman and others who endorse no-fault as a means of letting people represent themselves are in for a disappointment. But must lawyers be involved in divorce? Some people apparently think not. "Do-it-yourself" divorce kits are currently being sold in many states, particularly those which have some sort of no-fault ground. The kits consist of forms and instruction booklets (one uses long-playing records) and cost usually from thirty to one hundred dollars. Most kits are put out by nonlawyers. In New York, for instance, James Winder, a Rochester barber, has sold thousands at seventy-five dollars apiece. He used a lawyer himself when his first marriage was annulled some time ago. Since then, he read the New York divorce law, translated it to everyday English, and went into business. The Monroe County Bar Association, along with the Attorney General's office, obtained an injunction forbidding Winder from engaging in any activity "related directly or indirectly to matrimonial law or the procedure of the State of New York." The court's order was based on its finding that Winder was practicing law without a license. Ultimately the injunction was modified to allow him to write a do-it-yourself book, provided that he does not publish it himself or have any contact with his readers.

Bar associations are nervous about this kind of competition, but their efforts to put Winder and his fellows out of business are not necessarily self-protective. The legal profession is usually given the responsibility of preventing the unauthorized practice of law. This duty to police itself can raise problems of conflict of interest. It may not be clear which is the prevailing motivation: protecting the public against charlatans or driving out the competition. But the organized bar is not alone in fighting the do-it-yourself plans. Mrs. Harriet Gross, president of the Committee for Fair Divorce and Alimony Laws, charges that the "system of selling divorce kits to laymen is strictly a 'get-rich scheme' for the inventors, who are solely interested in self-aggrandizement." She adds that the kits can "cause enduring hardship in the areas of alimony, child support, child custody, taxes, visitation rights, property rights, and heavy legal costs to correct the errors of the do-it-yourselfer."

In Nevada, the husband of a former court employee put together an eighty-seven dollar divorce kit, but some judges refused to grant divorces to people who used it, ruling that the people's interests were not being adequately protected. In time an injunction was issued against the sale of the kit. Similar cases have arisen in other states. According to Bob Foss, a spokesman for the Florida Bar Association, "We've had some problems in the past with divorce kit firms. The kits themselves weren't necessarily unethical, but the people handing them out were. Some firms had been filling out forms for their customers; and some of the public, when we filed suit, protested that the bar was motivated by self-interest."

The divorce kits vary greatly in their quality, but even the best are risky. What may be good advice for most people can be costly for others, and it often takes a lawyer to know into which category a person falls. As Louise Raggio puts it, "Handling your own divorce is a little like taking out your own tonsils — it's a fairly routine operation, but you'd better let a professional handle it." In a way, it is a Catch-22 problem: you need a lawyer to tell you whether you need a lawyer. In most instances, the basic need is there. Court procedures can and should be simplified, but the complicated questions of divorce have always centered around issues of property and parental responsibilities rather than proving the grounds. Even when both spouses have agreed to divorce and have worked out a financial settlement, an attorney should probably check the arrangement for its tax consequences. Because one spouse's financial gain is usually the other's loss, disagreements about property are common. Unless the parties are equally strong and knowledgeable, they should be represented professionally in their bargaining.

If a lawyer is ordinarily needed, must you then pay eight hundred dollars — the figure that Denman calls a "swindle" — for a routine operation? The answer is no. Lawyers' fees are negotiable. If you are thinking about retaining a lawyer, do not be shy about asking how much he is going to charge. There is a wide variation in fees, but the cost should not be the sole criterion for picking a lawyer. You should have an attorney you respect — one you trust to handle your problems in a professional manner.

Attorneys are not allowed to advertise their specialties, and many do not handle domestic problems, so it is not always easy to find a good divorce lawyer. That an attorney takes only divorce cases, however, does not necessarily recommend him; you might not want a lawyer who would take an assembly-line approach to your case. On the other hand, Brooks Potter notes, "Divorce is a specialty if it's going to be handled properly. It isn't complicated, it doesn't require any genius like patent law to be a divorce lawyer, but you do have to be a semi-psychiatrist in order to understand people's needs. If you see a lawyer in court who has no divorce experience, it is pathetic the way he manhandles his client's affairs. Of course, it's also scandalous the way that some lawyers who've been around a long time play fast and loose with their clients' welfare." Paul Bohannan adds, "Perhaps there is no other situation in our country today in which a person in emotional distress is so faced with buying a pig in a poke. Clients who are inexperienced may not realize that they can fire a lawyer faster than they can hire him. They worry along with a lawyer they neither like personally nor trust professionally." If you do not already have a lawyer, you can turn to a clergyman, social service agency, or bar association, most of whom maintain referral lists; and if you fall below certain income guidelines, you can get help from a legal aid office.

It is not advisable (and in many states, it is not permissible) to have one lawyer represent both the husband and wife. In any divorce there are inherently conflicting interests which should be represented by different attorneys. The husband commonly pays the fees of both lawyers. This so offended one man in Baltimore that he chose to spend his nights and weekends in jail rather than pay. Nathaniel Denman contends that the rule of the Massachusetts courts which requires the husband to pay the legal fees in every case violates the equal protection clause of the Constitution, and he is trying to have it thrown out on that ground. Should he succeed, it will be only a moral victory. A number of states have modified their laws to make them sexless, that is, to provide that the "principal wage-earner" pay the legal fees of the "nonworking spouse." In almost all cases this would mean that the husband would still be responsible for his wife's legal expenses.

Some states have laws that make sure that lawyers get paid by somebody. Arizona, for example, has an unusual statute that provides that a divorce is not official until the lawyer files certain papers, even if the judge has already declared that the marriage is terminated. One attorney, V. L. Hask, used to warn all his clients, "You're not divorced until this decree is filed and it's not going to be filed until I'm paid." Most of his clients believed him, but apparently some did not. When Hask died in 1972 almost two hundred unfiled decrees were found, some dating back to the 1920s. One man, who thought he had been divorced three times, had not been officially divorced at all. The Arizona Supreme Court ultimately cleared up the mess by unilaterally calling all the divorces valid, but not before many of Hask's former clients had spent some anxious months worrying about bigamy and its ramifications.

# Chapter Eight

# The Politics of Reform

When the California legislature was considering divorce reform, only one religious group adamantly opposed the no-fault proposal made by the Governor's Commission on the Family. Undaunted by the broad support given the recommendations, it insisted that no new law compromise one of the principal tenets of its faith. The group? The Christian Science Church.

According to Richard Dinkelspiel, a cochairman of the commission, "The Christian Scientists were the only church group that had any objection. They were afraid that our conciliation program constituted compulsory psychiatric treatment, and they were opposed, of course, to any kind of mandatory medical procedure. Ultimately they were satisfied that we weren't proposing any such thing, so they were no longer opposed."

The response of the Catholic Church, on the other hand, ranged from surprising support to official indifference. An editorial in Sacramento's diocesan newspaper called it the "most constructive legislation before California lawmakers this session . . ." and the San Francisco archdiocese echoed this endorsement. Dinkelspiel notes that "the office of the cardinal in Los Angeles took no stand one way or the other. The important thing is that they didn't buck us."

In retrospect it seems that some of the Catholic enthusiasm may have been premature. For example, the Sacramento editorial gave prime attention to the proposed creation of family courts as well as the plan to make counseling mandatory in all the counties, but neither of these provisions was enacted by the legislature. The editorial also praised the abolition of the old divorce grounds, such as adultery and extreme cruelty, predicting that the adoption of a marriage breakdown standard would mean that courts "no longer would be divorce mills, grinding out civil dissolutions on request." The legislature did create an irreconcilable-differences ground, but California courts have not used it as a means to delve into the true state of the marriage. The *McKim* case notwithstanding, divorce has been available virtually on demand.

The history of divorce reform in California shows that the stereotypes do not always fit. The political battle lines are drawn differently in each state. The Catholic Church has vigorously opposed reform elsewhere, but went along with it in California, and thus made its adoption there easier. Likewise, family lawyers in some states are an active lobby for change, while in others they have worked against it. The California experience also reveals the extent of misinformation and miscalculation that usually accompanies the debate on no-fault divorce. Misconceptions about no-fault can cut both ways. They can cause some people to oppose change when they should really support it, and they can lead others to back it though it actually may be against their interest.

Because the factions and even the issues vary from state to state, it is difficult to generalize about the politics of divorce reform, but some common elements are apparent. The most important involves the underlying dynamics of reform. Across the country there seems to be a sense that our divorce laws are outmoded and serve no useful purpose. Whether or not this proposition can be scientifically proven — public opinion polls on such issues as divorce are of dubious value — it does seem as if only a minority of the population is steadfastly opposed to any revision of the laws. People may not be sure about what must be done, but there is a general feeling that reform is in order. This sentiment prevails not just in the United States. Brigitte Bodenheimer noted in her description of the public hearings preceding the enactment of the new Canadian divorce law that "the politicians lagged behind in their assessment of the public mood . . . one church organization after another and other witnesses were ahead of the thinking of some of the legislators." If public opinion favors divorce reform, why has it been so slow in coming? As should become clear in this chapter, it is largely because the opposition, though small, is far better organized — and in some instances more powerful — than the majority supporting change.

The lag between public opinion and legislative action also stems from the tendency to consider divorce more of a personal problem than a political issue, at least by most of those who are dissatisfied with the present system. Those who have recently gone through a divorce or are in the process of doing so are usually preoccupied with their individual troubles, not with broad social issues. The rest of us may shake our heads at the sorry state of the law, but on our lists of immediate priorities, divorce reform may rank relatively low. Perhaps this reflects an "it can't happen to us" attitude or a fear that thinking about divorce in the abstract may somehow make it more likely in reality.

There may also be a stigma of sorts attached to advocating divorce reform. One does not have to apologize for opposing water pollution, but a married person who starts to champion divorce reform is likely to get at least a raised eyebrow from his or her spouse and friends. By contrast, those who oppose reform are less likely to be suspected of grinding a personal ax; they can state their objections in terms of social considerations. Because such objections often arise from religious convictions or professional interests, they can be voiced through established organizations. Catholics who oppose divorce reform do not have to create a special lobbying group to advance their views, while proponents of change usually have to organize before they can make their weight felt.

Although public opinion may generally favor change, many politicians feel that supporting divorce reform is likely to cost them votes, and, in some cases, they may be right. Unless a politician has been conspicuous in his opposition to reform, he is unlikely to alienate the majority that favors it. But if he is a leader for change, those who are opposed may well punish him at the polls. As a result, many proposals for revision of the divorce laws get lost in a legislative committee or are sent down a dead-end road to a study commission. Legislators often find that ducking the divorce issue is the safest course in that it satisfies those who want to preserve the status quo, without unduly antagonizing those who want change. Reform thus sits on a back burner until some catalyzing action or event forces politicians to commit themselves publicly one way or the other.

In short, political opposition to divorce reform is not overwhelming; rather, support for it is diffuse. The call for change rarely comes from the public at large, because its views are not deeply felt; nor does it usually come from the legislators. Instead it has tended to come from smaller interest groups. The legal profession, or more precisely certain elements within it, sometimes has been an instigator of change. According to Herma Kay, "the drive to reform divorce law originated in California with the lawyers who handle divorce cases. The pressure to find an accommodation between felt needs and unyielding laws has fallen most heavily upon the professionals whose craftsmanship is essential to produce the desired result."

Although lawyers were active in the push for reform in California, this has not always been the case in other states. As mentioned in the preceding chapter, some lawyers oppose no-fault because they are afraid it would hurt their practices. There are other reasons for the bar's ambivalence about divorce reform. Robert Drinan, who was the editor of the *Family Law Quarterly* before entering Congress, once wrote, "Despite the basic unsuitability of America's present divorce procedure, borrowed from the ecclesiastical courts, little if any imagination has been exercised in the creation of a better process. The fact is that the American bench and bar have never really been interested in the law of domestic relations. Lawyers have tended to avoid divorce cases and have allowed a 'divorce bar' to grow up in each metropolitan area. Similarly judges, at least until very recently, have acquiesced in the fact that the divorce court enjoys the least prestige of all the courts."

Family law has been a legal backwater. There is little professional prestige for those who practice it or, for that matter, write about it. Yet attitudes do change. While John Kennedy was in Congress, he looked down his nose at the governorship of Massachusetts, saying, "I hate to think of myself up in that corner office deciding sewer contracts." Now that the sparkle has rubbed off foreign affairs and environmental problems seem more pressing, his judgment does not seem as obviously correct as it once did. Some law students are now turning away from the traditional goal of high-powered corporate law in favor of legal services or small-town practice, both of which involve a high proportion of family problems. If this phenomenon persists, there may be a growing interest in family law and a resulting awareness of its shortcomings, but it could be years before this in turn builds into pressure for change.

Louise Raggio found while trying to locate financial support for the efforts to revise Texas' family laws that apathy within the legal profession, not outright opposition, is presently the biggest obstacle to reform. "Nobody really cares about children and families. It makes for good talk, but that's all you get. When it comes down to making a real contribution, the insurance lawyers will work on the insurance code and the banking lawyers will work on the banking code, but who in the dickens is going to work on the family code? There is no money in it for anybody, so people don't want to donate their efforts." That she and her colleagues finally succeeded shows that her statement is hyperbole, but her underlying point is still valid.

Ignorance among lawyers is almost as big a problem as apathy. Many attorneys do not know enough about present divorce laws to make an intelligent judgment as to how they should be revised. A survey of the members of the Missouri Bar Association asked them how they wished to see the divorce laws changed. The results seemed to indicate general support for reform, but it was based on a surprisingly hazy understanding of the law. For example, ninety-one percent of those responding stated that they thought a judge should be able to grant a divorce even if both spouses have been guilty of marital misconduct. Yet in answer to another question in the same poll, forty-six percent said that they favored retaining the doctrine of recrimination. These results contradict each other. As explained in the first chapter, the doctrine of recrimination provides that there cannot be a divorce where both parties are at fault; thus by answering "yes" to the first question, ninety-one percent were saying in effect that recrimination should be abolished. The survey is also interesting in that it shows that lawyers, like most other people, are willing to state opinions even when they do not really grasp the issues.

There are other indications that not all lawyers are familiar with family law. *Boston Globe* reporter Bruce McCabe said that after he wrote a series of articles on divorce, he was contacted by many attorneys who wanted to know where they could learn more about the laws. He concluded, "The bars have got to take responsibility for de-mystifying divorce. They might start with their own membership."

In short, whether out of their apathy, ignorance, or hostility, lawyers cannot be relied on to reform the system on their own. In some states exceptionably able and hard-working attorneys have taken the lead, and in others bar associations have been sufficiently progressive to generate interest in reforming divorce laws. Such efforts are all to the good, but they are more the exception than the rule. If effective pressure for change is to come, it must come from some place else.

Although legislators, lawyers, and the general public have not generally taken the initiative in demanding revision of the laws, that has not left a complete vacuum. More and more divorced people are banding together to lobby for change. The groups that they formed have received notoriety, but for the most part they have not been taken seriously by the legal and political establishments. Judge Ralph Podell, for instance, dismisses most members as "borderline kooks." It is easy to concur with his diagnosis, for many of their tactics seem calculated more to generate newspaper copy for slow days than to persuade us of the serious need for reform.

Paul Hansen, the founder of Fathers United for Equal Rights, a Maryland organization, received national publicity for picketing in front of the church of a Baltimore judge. Hansen wore nothing but his underwear and a wooden barrel and carried signs that said "This Could Happen to You" and "Judge McGuire Repent." Hansen, a college English professor, cut a preposterous figure, but he claims that he was deadly serious. "Writing letters to the editor or appealing to judges gets you nowhere. Picketing in a barrel may seem silly, but it got us widespread publicity and lots of new members." Apparently he is right. In a period of less than two years, his organization has grown from just a handful to many hundreds. He has received inquiries from men throughout the country, but has limited membership to Maryland men, advising others to start similar organizations in their own states; in many cases they have.

By using stunts like Hansen's barrel or by appearing on radio talk shows, a few men have put out the call to other disgruntled ex-husbands. It is usually money, or more accurately the lack of it, that brings them together. Most of the men who get involved in such groups feel they came out on the short end of their divorces. Some blame their lawyers, others accuse the courts, and still others think that the entire system is unfair. Hansen attacks all three. "The laws stink, the lawyers are putrid, and the judges are so slow to change."

Members of groups like Hansen's commonly complain about the practice of requiring the husband to pay his wife's attorney, the specter of alimony jail, and the difficulty a man encounters if he wants custody of his children. The concerns of most of the men are genuine and deeply felt, but when the groups meet, more time seems to be spent exchanging tales of past personal suffering than working out ways to improve the divorce system for others. As a member of one Boston organization put it, "I'm sure everybody is in favor of reform and is dedicated to it, but the average guy sitting at this table, the average guy walking down the street, is interested in how he can best use this lousy system today, not two or three years from now. No-fault may be a wonderful thing, but it is just as separate from our problems as playing chess or going dancing."

Hansen believes that efforts at divorce reform are most productive if they are directed at a local, rather than national, level. Both because the laws and practices vary so much from state to state and the cost of maintaining a national organization is prohibitive, he has limited his attention to Maryland. "Effectiveness is really local effectiveness. You can monitor judges, picket them, and hang them in effigy in front of the bar association, and that gets them upset. They want to be treated as honorable men, but most are low-grade political hacks who knew somebody and got a job. Unfortunately it takes some kind of gimmick to make an impression on such people. Maybe you can't change their fundamental attitudes, but we've had good luck in getting them to change their conduct in the courtroom and that's what counts."

Most divorce reform groups are dominated by men who feel that they have been wounded by alimony and are not about to consort with the sex they think profits from it. The very name Fathers United for Equal Rights hints that men are oppressed and women are the oppressors. At first Hansen completely banned women from his organization, because he feared they would turn it into a "man-hunting social club." He later found that many of his members had remarried and their "second wives are being sucked dry financially." As a result, he created the Second Wives Coalition as a separate sister organization. In Massachusetts the recently founded Fathers United for Equal Justice does admit women, but relatively few have joined. Undoubtedly many have been turned off by the name and the orientation it suggests.

A divorced woman, who had come to her first meeting of Divorce Reform, Inc., in Boston, left after an hour and said that she would not bother to come again. "They are bitter men and they have real complaints, but nobody is listening to them. Yet they don't seem to listen either. A whole lot of women get hurt by divorce too." The woman had come both because she was interested in divorce reform and because she wanted to "meet some new men," but she was disappointed on each count. "I suppose they have to get rid of their hostility — misery loves company — but that's not what I'm looking for."

It would be a mistake to write off all such groups as male-dominated therapy sessions. Ray Fletz, the chairman of the Minnesota State Bar Association's Family Law Committee, reports that his organization has surveyed the various groups in that state and has found that "some of them have reached the stage of maturity where we have had to acknowledge the wisdom of their proposals, so we can now start working with them as a resource." In New York, Alimony, Ltd., was founded a decade ago by several men who wanted to abolish alimony. It has since changed its name to Fair Divorce and Alimony Laws, greatly expanded its membership, and elected a woman president. The group has carried on some flamboyant picketing, but it has also worked in quieter ways to develop effective influence with lawmakers in Albany.

There are other groups, such as Parents Without Partners, whose principal efforts so far have been to help divorced people to adjust to their new lives, rather than to lobby for law reform. Some lawyers say that such outfits are "fleshmarkets, a dating service without the expense of a computer," but these remarks are unfair. Divorce can be painful in practical and emotional terms, and cooperative effort can sometimes alleviate the problems. Many church and adult education programs have organized similar groups on a smaller scale. Their membership may be an untapped source of support for divorce reform.

In the last several years criticism of the divorce laws has begun to come from a different quarter. Leaders of the women's movement who have challenged traditional roles in marriage have also considered the implications of divorce. If marriage can be oppressive, it might seem logical to call for easier divorce so that women can free themselves from their bonds; but, as Herma Kay has noted, some feminists have become increasingly critical of liberalized divorce laws. "It has been suggested, for example, that since married women [housewives] work not for pay but for security— that is, the expectation of continued support from their husbands — that divorce is therefore against the interests of women."

Much feminist criticism of present divorce laws centers around financial matters, rather than on the issue of grounds. As pointed out in Chapter Four, there is convincing evidence that alimony and child support awards are often insufficient to begin with and frequently go unpaid. Attempts to limit alimony to a period of rehabilitation may be appropriate for some women, but they overlook the fact that many middle-aged women, though willing to work, are unable to find jobs. Indeed, when men like Nathaniel Denman and Paul Hansen say the courts are "biased" against males or that the laws are "putrid," they ignore the fact that males wrote the laws and males enforce them. In Massachusetts, for example, only five of the state's two hundred and eighty legislators are women. Only three percent of the state's judges and fewer than ten percent of the lawyers are female. If divorce laws are unfair to men, it would seem that men have only themselves to blame.

Carol Bangs, one of the founders of Justice for Divorced and Separated Mothers, a Cambridge, Massachusetts, group, believes that far from being biased against men, the divorce laws are detrimental to women, especially those with children. "A husband can run off and leave his wife and children with no money; if she has spent her life being prepared to be a housewife and a mother, she may not be able to find work. Theoretically, her husband owes her support, but the law puts the burden on her to get it. She has to hire a lawyer to collect what is due her, and if the husband skips off to another state, it is usually too much trouble to go after him. It seems like a system designed to protect the guilty."

She helped to found her organization out of the hope of changing that system, but, after several years of hard work, she is pessimistic about accomplishing much in the near future. It is difficult for unmarried mothers, who in addition to caring for children often must work, to make time to push for divorce reform. Moreover, many of the members have come to feel that the problems they encounter are larger than the written divorce laws. Carol Bangs says, "The refusal of society to do anything about divorce reform reflects the belief that it is the woman's fault if the marriage breaks up, because women are supposedly responsible for emotional relationships. Then we also have to overcome the stereotype that women are out to soak their ex-husbands for a lot of money." Her group has started to prepare a manual, tentatively titled *Divorce Karate*, that will advise women how to use the existing laws to protect themselves, but a lack of money has slowed its work. MOMMA, a similar organization in the Los Angeles area, has gotten further off the ground. It publishes an informative monthly magazine — also called *MOMMA* — distributed throughout the country.

The present divorce system is not biased in favor of either sex. In different ways, it is unfair to men, women, and children; one person's loss is not always another's gain. The inequities seem to fall particularly heavily on women. For example, the laws of many states provide that it is the husband's right to choose the family domicile. If a man wants to move to a new area and his wife does not wish to leave her friends and relatives or her work, he can divorce her for desertion, but she cannot divorce him. Much of this sort of inequity stems from the archaic laws governing marriage. Because a wife cannot choose her own legal domicile, she is supposed to vote where her husband does; similarly, if she marries an out-of-stater, she may be denied residents' privileges at her home state university. Attempts to rectify these kinds of problems often lead women indirectly into divorce reform. The Texas divorce law was changed in the course of a sweeping revision of the family laws that had begun because of dissatisfaction with the out-moded marital property laws. Diana DuBroff founded the National Organization to Insure Support Enforcement to protect children, but her work has led her to realize that broader reform of divorce laws is also needed. Many of the women who worked for divorce reform in California were particularly concerned with giving wives more control over community property during marriage and more rights after divorce.

Many feminists feel the problems of divorce cannot be solved simply by revising the grounds for divorce. Regina Healy, a legal services lawyer in Cambridge, says, "Perhaps I'll change my mind, but I think that no-fault divorce may be a non-issue. Sure, the fault system is degrading when it makes a woman go before the court and state that she has been cruelly treated; she has to appear helpless. I suppose that ought to be eliminated, but in perspective, the damage done by that fifteen minutes of embarrassment in court is nothing compared to the harm that arises from the economic position most people find themselves in. We presume in this country that there should be only one wage earner for a family, and this presumption puts everyone in a tenuous position. The wife and children are completely dependent on the husband, and he is stuck with what may be an unbearable burden. What seems to be called for is a redistribution, not just of income, but of the source of income. Economics is the central issue; divorce law is really secondary."

The kinds of changes which Carol Bangs, Regina Healy, and others feel are necessary to lessen the hardship of divorce for women involve marriage and property laws, employment and educational policies, and fundamental attitudes about sex roles. Carol Bangs says, "Men who feel that alimony and child support are punishment are wrong, but I can understand why they react that way. While they were married, they never had to take a specific, agreed-on sum out of their paychecks to cover these costs, so when they are divorced, it comes as quite a shock. If a wife were paid for the work she does in the home, then there would be far fewer financial problems should the marriage have to end." She recognizes that it will take many years to alter popular attitudes about divorce, because they depend on ingrained conceptions about the responsibilities of marriage. Until there is such a change, divorced women must cope with the system — fault or no-fault — as it exists. Justice for Divorced and Separated Mothers has not accomplished as much in this regard as its founders had hoped. MOMMA and other groups may be more successful in providing services to divorced women, as well as in lobbying for change.

Divorce reform has come slowly because its potential constituency is fragmented. Fathers United for Equal Justice and Justice for Divorced and Separated Mothers both hold their regular meetings in Cambridge, but it is impossible to imagine the two groups ever merging. Their experiences, goals, and manners are quite different. Although they will never work side-by-side, their independent activities have jointly contributed to a growing public awareness of some of the problems of divorce. They have brought out in the open different aspects of an issue which not long ago was considered taboo.

The times can be right for change and opinion can favor it, but a spark is needed to get it started. Until 1966 New York's law, allowing divorce only for adultery, had been virtually unchanged since it was written by Alexander Hamilton. It had been criticized for many years, but serious efforts at reform did not begin until Governor Nelson Rockefeller received a Nevada divorce in 1962. The impact of the Rockefeller divorce was threefold. It dramatized the unfairness of a system which allowed wealthy people to get divorced by taking a six-week vacation in Nevada, while average people were stuck in New York with the unattractive choice of faking an adultery scene or simply deserting their spouse. That he was easily reelected in his next campaign for governor also showed that the public was more willing to accept divorce than most politicians had imagined. And finally, Rockefeller's divorce meant that he himself was in no position to oppose reform. Divorce reform groups tried to make him a symbol of their cause by picketing his mansion and demanding that he take a progressive stand. An official of the National Council of Churches asserted that because Rockefeller had "connived to avoid the laws he swore to uphold," he was obligated to push for laws "more equitable for people who can't afford to go to Nevada." Rockefeller did call the New York law "archaic," but he said that it was the legislature's job, not his, to formulate a new one.

In 1964 the Association of the Bar of the City of New York began a concerted drive for divorce reform. According to its then president, Samuel Rosenman, the bar was troubled by the high incidence of out-of-state divorces that were taking place "only because of the very limited and restricted grounds on which a divorce may be granted here." Because the validity of divorce decrees from some other states and countries was somewhat in question, the association feared that many New Yorkers who thought they had been divorced were, in fact, still married to their first spouses, and thus involved in complex problems of bigamy, illegitimacy, and inheritance. The *New York Times* added its weight to the reform movement with sympathetic stories and editorials. During this same period, the validity of quickie Mexican divorces was being litigated. New York's highest court upheld them, so long as both parties had consented and one of them had actually gone to Mexico. No minimum time had to be spent there; a morning was good enough. The court's decision made the New York divorce statute seem all the more ridiculous, since it could be circumvented by anyone who could afford to fly to Juarez. The press also pointed out that many people who had canny lawyers, a little luck, and perhaps some influence were getting around the supposedly strict law by having their marriages annulled.

In 1965 the legislature responded to these pressures by creating a Joint Committee on Matrimonial and Family Law; its chairman, Jerome Wilson, a young, somewhat abrasive state senator, made sure that the divorce issue did not die there. A parade of prominent citizens and representatives of church groups testified to the need for a revised law. Erwin Griswold, then Dean of Harvard Law School and later the Solicitor-General of the United States, stated that when a marriage is dead, the law should recognize it. "To my mind this is not a religious question. There are persons who are opposed to divorce on religious grounds and I fully respect their views. But we have a clear separation of church and state in this country. Under our legal and constitutional system, one person should not bind another through the law." Soon after John Lindsay was elected mayor of New York, he announced his support for reform.

Up to this point the leadership of the Catholic Church had taken a low profile on the divorce issue, confident that it could use its political influence quietly to preserve the status quo, but the gathering momentum forced it out in the open. Charles Tobin, Jr., a lobbyist for some of the bishops in the state, told the legislative committee that because "the quality of permanence is the very essence of marriage," the bishops would "oppose changing the grounds for divorce so as to broaden them in such a way that the government would, in effect, be permitting a procedure tantamount to divorce by consent."

Catholics, however, did not unanimously adhere to this position. A number of Catholic judges had already testified in favor of reform, and, within several months of Tobin's statement, Senator Robert Kennedy called the existing laws unfair and contrary to the proper administration of justice. His sister, Patricia Kennedy Lawford, had just received an Idaho divorce, which again underscored the duality of the law. At the same time, a group of leading Catholic politicians and public figures announced the organization of a lay group to support reform.

The Catholic leadership was put on the defensive. Tobin responded with a letter, that was distributed to all Catholic legislators, asking for a moratorium on any change in the law until more information on divorce was available. The *Times* editorially criticized the letter as a stall, and Senator Wilson used stronger language. He called it "seemingly a declaration of war" on meaningful divorce reform and while on the Senate floor stated, "Mr. Tobin has killed divorce reform in the State of New York. He cannot be allowed to do it again." Wilson was bitterly rebuked by some of his colleagues who did not like the suggestion that their votes could be manipulated by an outsider. Some swore they would never vote for a bill with his name on it, and others who favored reform felt that Wilson's intemperate remarks were an uncalled-for obstacle to compromise. In retrospect, however, Wilson claimed that his statement had a positive effect. "It was a deliberate act intended to produce certain results and it produced those results." Wilson felt that since public opinion had been demonstrated clearly to favor reform, it was necessary to force his colleagues to make a conspicuous stand. His tactic may have been correct. The reform movement had been stuck, and his comments, together with other factors, helped break the logjam.

A compromise, described in Chapter Six, was finally worked

out whereby the Church went along with allowing people to divorce after living apart for two years, and the reformers accepted a provision that purported to make a conciliation hearing a prerequisite for any divorce. It turned out to be a poor deal for the Catholics. The legislature soon cut the separation period to one year. The conciliation bureaus — which the legislature has now tried to eliminate altogether — have been so understaffed that most people have satisfied the statutory requirement simply by answering a three-page questionnaire. In spite of the heated debate and long delay, the compromise version of the divorce bill passed with astonishing ease, by votes of one hundred and fifty-seven to seven in the Assembly and sixty-four to one in the Senate.

Not all reform movements are sparked from a desire to liberalize the divorce laws. The genesis of the no-fault law in California was, if anything, just the opposite. When Governor Edmund Brown created his Commission on the Family in 1966, he instructed it to conduct a "concerted assault on the high incidence of divorce in our society," but ironically the end result of the commission's work was a statute under which the number of divorces has increased almost fifty percent. Obviously something happened between the time Brown gave the commission its mandate and the time the law was passed. Instead of curing the problem of the rising divorce rate, reform exacerbated it.

Much of the explanation lies in the legislative process. Although the commission had spent several years of careful study before it submitted its final recommendations, the legislature properly held its own hearings on the reform bill. Some of the provisions came under heavy fire, particularly the requirement of an initial conciliation conference for every couple seeking a divorce. This plan and the proposed creation of special family courts were ultimately rejected by the legislature, apparently out of an unfounded fear of the cost. Conciliation was intended to be only a screening mechanism, but had it been made mandatory in all cases, the tone of the entire divorce procedure might have been quite different. No-fault divorce had been proposed as a means of getting away from the artificial and often irrelevant categories of adultery and cruelty; the breakdown approach was supposed to provide a meaningful inquiry into the viability of each marriage. For better or worse, however, there have been no such inquiries under the new California law; divorce has been available pretty much on demand. If a conciliation program had been created, more people might have been encouraged to reconsider their marriage problems; and this in turn might have led courts to take a more active role in determining whether irreconcilable differences do in fact exist. Had the legislature accepted the commission's conciliation proposal, the resulting statute might have come closer to accomplishing Brown's goal.

Those people who participated on the commission, however, do not regard their work as a failure. Richard Dinkelspiel notes that reform was actually "prompted by a lot of things: the divorce rate, the manner in which courts were handling divorce problems, the hypocrisy of designating grounds, the use of things that are shocking, like adultery and cruelty, as clubs to force property and custody concessions — all these things entered into it." Measured by these objectives, the commission was largely successful for the new statute has eliminated much of the hypocrisy and bitterness which used to be the by-products of divorce law. Nevertheless, it is interesting that divorce reform in California did not end up exactly where it initially was headed.

The emphasis to this point has been directed at the difficulty in getting the various elements of the population that are interested in divorce reform to coalesce into an effective constituency for change; this has been the principal reason why change has come so slowly. It has been less a case of the opposition's keeping the lid on reform than it has been a matter of the proponents' not being able to generate enough steam to blow the lid off. That is not to say, however, that opposition to divorce reform can be entirely ignored, for when reform movements have gathered strength, the opposition has often been smoked out into the open and accommodations have had to be made.

Often the opposition is religious, particularly Catholic, but, as seen in California, there have been instances when even the Catholic Church has actively supported divorce reform. There have been other instances, of course, when the Church has stymied change. There are several explanations for this apparent schizophrenia. As is becoming increasingly evident in other areas, the Church is not the monolithic entity it is often imagined to be. Also, the posture of the Church depends on the situation it faces in a given state. In California, the divorce laws were already so liberally interpreted the Church could not easily assume the role of the defender of the status quo. In spite of the hypocrisy and inequities, divorce was easy to obtain, so from the Church's point of view, any change seemed likely to be one for the better. As it turned out, the irreconcilable-differences standard became a euphemism for divorce on demand. Had this been apparent from the outset, the Catholic press probably would not have been so enthusiastic about the proposed changes in the law.

There have also been instances where the Church has supported, or at least tolerated, the revision of divorce laws which had been applied conservatively. The Catholic Women's League of Canada testified in legislative hearings that its members did not wish to force their own religious beliefs about the sanctity of marriage on the rest of Canadian society. Canada's organization of bishops publicly stated that Catholic legislators were not obliged to oppose reform of the divorce laws and were permitted "out of respect for freedom of conscience, to tolerate a revision of existing divorce legislation with a view to obviating present abuses." Although the Church was careful to caution against "indiscriminate broadening of the grounds for divorce," its action paved the way for progressive change.

Some Catholic leaders like the late Cardinal Cushing of Boston have stressed that their Church has no desire to impose its precepts on social issues like birth control on the rest of the public. "It is important to note that Catholics do not need the support of civil law to be faithful to their religious convictions and they do not seek to impose by law their morals on other members of society." Yet such admonitions are not always heeded within the structure of the Church. When the Massachusetts legislature was considering making divorce available to couples who had mutually separated for one year, Monsignor Paul Harrington, presiding judge of the Metropolitan Tribunal of the Archdiocese of Boston, invoked religious arguments in opposition. "The concept of divorce by mutual agreement, without alleging or proving any cause, is based on the fiction that every married couple has a right to a dissolution when either one becomes disenchanted by a marriage and has a right to the easiest and speediest procedure possible with the least inconvenience." Monsignor

Harrington stated that such a "fiction" could not be further from the truth, because "marriage was divinely instituted as a permanent and indissoluble union between one man and one woman for better or for worse throughout their natural life-time and a union that can only be dissolved by death."

Monsignor Harrington's conception of divinely instituted marriage would seem to be just that sort of "religious conviction" that Cardinal Cushing warned his fellow Catholics not to impose on the rest of society. In Massachusetts, however, Monsignor Harrington's approach has prevailed, and the conservative influence of the Church in the state legislature has been strong. Representative Cornelius Kiernan, the chairman of the House Judiciary Committee, is a Catholic bachelor who has little patience for divorce reformers; thus far, the no-fault bills which have passed through his committee have been reported out unfavorably and heavily defeated on the floor.

The political strength of the Church — and its inclination to use it — varies from state to state. In Michigan it was unable to muster much opposition to no-fault and had to settle simply for making its negative feelings known. After the Michigan Senate passed the no-fault bill, one of the Catholic members warned his colleagues, "When the divorce rate sky-rockets, when immorality becomes commonplace, when the taxpayers revolt in disgust at the ever increasing A.D.C. and welfare rolls caused by broken homes, when our court systems become even further behind in handling huge case loads of custody, support, and property disputes caused by this bill, do not say you were not warned of the consequences — for surely society as a whole will pay dearly for the passage of this bill here today. . . ." In spite of these gloomy predictions, Governor William Milliken signed the bill into law.

In Connecticut, the state bar association's Family Law Committee was able to stimulate broad support for divorce reform from professional organizations, the press, and other church groups, but found that Catholic opposition to no-fault, though covert, was powerful. Committee chairman Samuel Schoonmaker says, "Our state is very Catholic, roughly forty-five percent, and Archbishop Whalen of Hartford is rather conservative. The Catholic opposition to reform has never been vocal. It works through its legislators. Until 1973 the chairmen of the judiciary committees of both houses were Catholics, so the no-fault bills that we submitted were reported out unfavorably." Both chairmen were replaced, and ultimately a reform bill was enacted; but the competing political forces tugged and pulled to such an extent that the original no-fault proposal of the bar association emerged twisted beyond recognition. One eminent law professor calls the new Connecticut statute a "hopeless mishmash"; it allows divorce for marital breakdown, eighteen months' separation, or the traditional fault grounds. The law seemingly includes something for everyone, but the confusion which is likely to arise may prove that the compromise was worse than any of the competing alternatives.

In some cases, the deals which are struck between the various political factions are at least palatable to all; such was the case in New York. In other instances, notably Connecticut, the compromises have been less admirable. The Catholic Church is often criticized for trying to force its religious convictions on the rest of society. Whether Griswold's suggestion that this threatens a violation of the separation of church and state is true depends on the way the issue of divorce reform is characterized. If it is seen as essentially a question of protecting the private right to marry and unmarry, then opposition by the Church may be meddlesome; but if broader social implications are raised, then the Catholics should have as much right as anyone else to use their political power to shape a society that is to their liking. In truth, divorce law has important ramifications for the individual and society; what kind of law we have is both a product of and an influence on our values. It is not inappropriate then for the Church and its followers to take a strong position on divorce reform, but unfortunately in most instances, much of the politicking has been behind the scenes rather than in full public view. While this is true for many political issues, of course, it is particularly disheartening that the values and principles involved in divorce reform cannot be discussed in free and open debate.

In one state that was considering no-fault several years ago, the family law section of the bar association was able to remove the Catholic roadblock by secretly promising that it would not later push for a liberalized abortion law. Officials of the Church do not like to acknowledge the deal, apparently because they are reluctant to admit that some of the Church's principles of faith are negotiable, and because the United States Supreme Court's later action in striking down existing antiabortion statutes made it an embarrassingly bad trade. Those who engineered the bargain for the bar association are in a position to gloat, but do not do so, since they know that they will have to sit down in the future to negotiate with the Church on other issues.

In short, the position of the Catholic Church on divorce reform varies from support in some states, to symbolic resistance in others, to entrenched opposition in still others. In general, it seems to prefer to use its influence quietly, though events and strong public sentiment for change can sometimes force it out in the open. Although its principles may seem inflexible, it has often been forced to make large compromises.

Family lawyers are the other principal opponents to reform. As pointed out in Chapter Seven, the legal profession is divided on the question of no-fault divorce. The great majority is apathetic. For many of those who are concerned, the line is usually drawn according to how they think no-fault would affect their own economic interest. San Francisco lawyer Tim Savinar is unusual only in his frankness. "I'm in a bind. I make money off divorce. It's just like no-fault automobile insurance: any change is against my personal interest. I guess I'm on the wrong end of all this stuff. At heart I don't see anything about the institution of marriage that should make it subject to the state, except for questions of property and child custody. Yet I have a personal interest in having everything handled in court."

Savinar and many attorneys like him would be pleased to see the status quo maintained, but they are not inclined to oppose actively any movement for further reform; they just are not about to lead it. There are some lawyers, however, who are willing to dig in their heels against change. To minimize their influence, any reform movement is wise to involve reputable members of the bar from the outset. In California, for example, the Governor's Commission on the Family was dominated by lawyers and law professors. Although their views may not necessarily have been representative of the state's divorce bar, their participation made it more difficult for the legal community to claim that it had been left out of the policy making. The commission was aware of potential opposition and took care to emphasize that lawyers would still be involved at every stage of the divorce process. Nevertheless, the board of governors of the state bar association opposed the reform bill as it was submitted, and their stand was ammunition for those who wanted to shoot down the provision creating family courts. In many states, the criticism by the officers of the bar association would have been fatal for the entire bill, but because the commission had framed its proposals so as to guard against an attack by the legal profession, the association's influence was largely blunted.

This tactic does not always succeed. A liaison committee from the Family Law Section of the A.B.A. was created to assist the drafters of the Uniform Marriage and Divorce Act, but many of the members of the committee came to believe that they were outsiders whose sole function was to be window dressing. That the committee largely felt that its opinions on policy were not heeded probably contributed to the later rift between the section and the commissioners.

In Michigan there was some jockeying between that state's Law Revision Commission and the bar association. The former advocated a wholesale revision of Michigan's family laws, while the latter was far less enthusiastic about change. Because the commission was bipartisan and generally well regarded, the power of the bar was correspondingly diminished; had it been inclined to fight for the status quo, it would have looked as if it were acting out of self-interest. Ultimately the bar agreed to the complete abolition of the fault grounds, a position that it probably would never have taken on its own initiative. The reform bill was passed by the Michigan legislature in one-sided votes, an indication of both the general weakness of the opposition and the deference paid to the Law Revision Commission.

When specific proposals are generated by existing commissions like Michigan's or by blue ribbon panels like California's, legislatures are likely to act favorably, though the bills which are ultimately passed may bear little resemblance to the original recommendations. In Texas and other states, reform has been led by the family law committees of the bar associations, but such organizations can have a much harder time selling their proposals, as they can make no claim that they are impartial representatives of society's interest. Regardless of what position a bar association advocates, it is vulnerable to the charge that it is acting out of self-interest.

In some cases the organized bar has been in no position to promote or fight divorce reform, whatever its desires might be. In Illinois, for instance, a series of exposés in the *Chicago Sun-Times* caused the legislature to call for an investigation of divorce lawyers and their practices; a committee with the power to subpoena witnesses was established. Although the investigation apparently turned up no wrongdoing, Stanton Ehrlich, a Chicago lawyer and former chairman of the Family Law Section of the A.B.A., thinks that the accusations of shady dealings had a negative impact. "They have seriously undermined, perhaps totally destroyed, all the efforts of the last twenty-five years to upgrade the image of the divorce lawyer, which has been near the bottom of the barrel since I was born. We had started to get someplace in terms of prestige, and now unfortunately we are back to where we began."

The Illinois state bar association created a one hundred and fifty–person committee in 1970 to consider rewriting the matrimonial laws, but in three years it has yet to formulate any recommendations. The Chicago Bar Association has endorsed a no-fault plan, and its action may force the state organization to take a stand. The political in-fighting that is going on between the two groups may be moot, however, as the Illinois divorce bar may not have the credibility with the public or the legislature to take an active part in the movement for reform, one way or the other.

Divorce reform does not follow the traditional political boundaries. It has been achieved in "liberal" states like California, Oregon, and Michigan, but it has also come about in "conservative" states like Texas, Iowa, and Vermont. Nor is it usually a party issue. To the extent that conventional politics and geography come into play, the Northeast seems a bit more conservative than the rest of the country, possibly because of a different history, a higher percentage of Catholics, and a somewhat less mobile population.

Sociologist Clinton Phillips sees the incidence of divorce and the pressure for reforming the laws as a reflection of a given state's culture. "In California we have a highly mobile, anonymous, transient, striving, thrill-seeking, experience-seeking population. All of this has an effect on the tendency toward easier divorce that has been growing since World War I. . . . I'm afraid that we're in for a lot of divorcing, at least in the transient, urban population." California is indeed a long way from Massachusetts, yet the sociological differences cannot be the sole reason why there is a liberal law in the former and a conservative one in the latter. Nebraska is not particularly urban or transient, yet like California it now has no-fault divorce.

The diversity of the states which have adopted no-fault indicates that the success or failure of reform depends in large part on the political skill and energy of the people who are behind it. Those who can draw together the diffuse elements of support succeed; those who cannot are usually blocked by the opposition. Complex questions of political strategy are involved; the opposition must be identified, drawn out, and dealt with.

There is also an element of luck required. California's Governor Ronald Reagan is opposed to what he conceives as "permissive" social legislation, but the fact that he himself had been divorced for extreme cruelty by his former wife Jane Wyman put him in a position where he had to sign — and perhaps wanted to — the new no-fault law. A lawyer from another state says, "We had been trying to reform the divorce laws for a number of years, but couldn't get the time of day from the legislative leadership. Then it just happened one year that several of them were in the midst of divorces and apparently they didn't like what they were experiencing, so our bill went through like gang-busters." An official of the bar association of an eastern state says, "The key to our getting no-fault was the fact that the chairman of the senate judiciary committee and the speaker of the house, who had both opposed us in the past, were in the middle of messy marital situations when we reintroduced our bill, and they switched right around."

In some instances it may be best to push for complete change of all the family laws; this was done in California and Texas. In some other states, like Michigan and Vermont, an incremental change has been called for. The chances for success and the appropriate strategy depend largely on the character of the existing law. In New York the statute that purported to allow divorce only in the case of adultery had been so circumvented by collusion, out-of-state decrees, and easy annulment that reform was almost inevitable. The issue was not so much between easy and difficult divorce as it was between hypocrisy and honesty. Legislators did not have to ask themselves what sort of laws they would draft from scratch for an ideal world, but rather whether they were satisfied with the status quo. The answer was clearly no. Reform thus can be more a rejection of an old system than it is an informed endorsement of no-fault divorce.

# Chapter Nine

# No-Fault and Quickie Divorce

In 1969 the Nevada Bar Association accused Reno attorney Howard McKissick, Jr., of telling the truth. After a careful investigation, it found him guilty; he was "censored," that is, officially chastised, for his indiscretion. McKissick had reportedly told some California legislators that if they passed the proposed Family Law Act, they would "ruin the Nevada divorce racket" and that Nevada divorce lawyers would "have to find something legitimate to do."

McKissick denied making those precise remarks, claiming that a newspaper reporter had misquoted him in a casual conversation. McKissick is known to be outspoken, but, given his professional background, his version of the incident may be correct. He is a divorce lawyer himself and has represented Marilyn Monroe, Nelson Rockefeller, Judy Garland, and a string of other celebrities. He also served in the Nevada legislature for seven terms, including one as Speaker of the Assembly.

Yet whether or not he made the comments is not the important point, for even if he did, they are very much the truth. The number of divorces in Nevada had been steadily declining through the nineteen-sixties, and it dropped another fifteen percent the year the new California law went into effect. Many Californians who used to go to Nevada to get divorced no longer found it worth the bother and expense, so they stayed home. The liberalization of divorce laws in California and other states has definitely hurt the incomes of Reno and Las Vegas family lawyers.

It was probably McKissick's reported use of the word "racket" to characterize Nevada divorce practice that particularly offended the elders of the bar association, but that term is the right one. For decades people have come to Nevada from New York, Massachusetts, and other states for quickie divorces. They have stayed on dude ranches the requisite six weeks, made brief appearances in the county courthouse, and sworn, under oath, that they were residents of Nevada and intended to remain there indefinitely. Several hours later, clutching their divorce papers, they have boarded planes to return home. In short, the Nevada divorce business has involved fraud coming and going. People who are barred by the laws of their own state from obtaining a divorce get around the prohibition by escaping to Nevada. Once there they falsely swear that they intend to remain. Reno divorces are indeed a racket, but a racket in which all involved willingly take part. The people are relieved to get their divorces, the lawyers are delighted to get their fees, and the Nevada judges go along with a system that produces substantial revenue for their state.

Migratory divorce, as it is called by lawyers, is not a new phenomenon. Before the turn of the century, Americans sought out the easiest states and, in some cases, countries in which to get divorced. Yet though "divorce mills" like Reno and Juarez have received a great deal of publicity, they have never accounted for anything close to a majority of American divorces; in recent years, such places are estimated to have produced fewer than ten percent of the total divorces granted to Americans.

Migratory divorce constitutes only a small fraction proportionately, but it has had a large impact on the development of family law. Attempts by New York and other states to restrict divorce for their citizens have been futile, or at least far less effective, because of the availability of Reno decrees. That migratory divorce has always been feasible for the rich, but not the poor, has demonstrated not only the hypocrisy, but the unfairness of restrictive laws, which fact, in turn, has helped to generate interest in reform. Thus, the very success that Reno and such places have enjoyed has ultimately contributed to their decline.

Most aspects of divorce law are relatively untechnical, but the rules regarding the validity of migratory divorces are unusually complex. It would be needlessly confusing to discuss them here in rigorous detail, but several basic principles should be explained. Two requirements generally must be met in order to have a valid. divorce. First, the particular state's residency statute must be satisfied; and, second, the person seeking the divorce must have established domicile in the state that grants the divorce.

As to the first requirement, each state may, within certain limits, fix a minimum period that a person must be in residence before he or she can be granted a divorce; generally speaking, residence is equivalent to physical presence. Even if a person has obvious grounds and there is no contest, he or she still must wait out the residency period before getting a divorce.

Nevada and Idaho have the shortest periods, six weeks, while other states have longer ones, ranging from sixty days to three years. Alabama has a one-year residency requirement in contested cases, but sets no minimum if the case is uncontested and both spouses appear in court. The length of the residency period is set by each state's legislature, but some recent federal court decisions have held that an unduly long time can be an unconstitutional violation of the equal protection clause. As a result, the residency requirements of several states have been thrown out; it is not clear yet just how long a period a state may legitimately require.

Although judges in quickie divorce states are often loose about other procedural matters, they are usually very strict in applying the residency provision. A Reno attorney was recently convicted on a perjury charge for allowing a divorce client to lie that he had been a resident of Nevada for six weeks when he actually had been in California most of the time. When people from out of state come to Reno for a divorce, they are usually accompanied in court by the desk clerk of the hotel or ranch at which they are staying; he testifies that they have been present for the full forty-two days. Judge Grant Bowen of the Washoe County Court in Reno says, "The general attitude is that if people are going to come here to take advantage of our divorce laws, then it is no hardship to require them to spend six weeks and spend a little money."

Satisfying the residency requirement is only the first step. The second involves the question of domicile and is somewhat more complicated. Article IV of the Constitution provides, among other things, that each state must give "Full Faith and Credit" to the public acts and judicial proceedings of all the other states. Although this language might seem to compel Massachusetts to recognize any divorce granted by a Nevada court, the United States Supreme Court has ruled that in order for a divorce decree of one state to command recognition by courts in other states, the person who sought the divorce must have been domiciled in the state which granted the divorce. Domicile is a somewhat elusive legal concept, but in essence it constitutes something more than mere residence. One need not live in a place permanently to acquire domicile, but there must be an intent to remain there some indefinite time.

If either of the spouses has established domicile in a state, then that state has the power to grant a divorce that must be respected by its sister states. Although judges in Nevada are strict when it comes to making sure that the residency requirement has been met, they are quite lax in regard to domicile. The divorce lawyer always asks, "Is it your intent to remain in the state of Nevada for an indefinite time?" The client invariably answers, "Yes," even though he or she probably has a ticket for a flight home that afternoon. One Nevada judge remembers having to schedule a court hearing early in the morning so that an all-pro quarterback could catch a plane to get him to training camp on time; the player has not been back to Nevada since then.

Does the full faith and credit clause require other states to honor the Nevada court's finding that domicile was established there? The Supreme Court has said that it does not. Although they must give the Nevada finding some "respect," they are not bound by it; thus by determining that domicile was not acquired, they can invalidate the divorce itself. Courts in some conservative states look very hard at out-of-state divorce decrees. The Massachusetts Appeals Court recently refused to recognize the Florida divorce of a man who had lived in that state for almost two years. Because he had been on leave of absence from his position with the Boston school system and had kept up payments on his home, the court said that he had intended all the while to return to Massachusetts. Although he clearly was a resident of Florida for two years, the court ruled that he had never been domiciled there; hence his divorce and second marriage were invalid.

In most instances, challenges to quickie divorces are brought by the spouse who was left behind. If the person who got the divorce does return to his home state, there is a very good chance that the divorce can be overturned. Even if the other spouse chooses not to challenge it, the divorce still may not be airtight. In a famous North Carolina case, a prosecutor attacked the validity of two Nevada divorces by bringing a bigamy charge against a couple who had divorced their first spouses in Nevada and then married each other. The North Carolina courts found that because neither person had established domicile in Nevada, their divorces were invalid; hence their marriage constituted bigamy. The state on its own initiative thus can use the criminal laws to discourage people from trying to circumvent its restrictive divorce laws.

Migratory divorce obviously does not provide a simple solution to somebody who wants to end his or her marriage. Unless legitimate domicile is established in the state that grants the divorce, it may easily be attacked when the person returns home. A person who wants to end a marriage cannot just pack his or her bags and head for Reno. Why then do so many people resort to migratory divorce? The answer lies in the legal principle, *res judicata.* If both the husband and wife participated in the out-of-state divorce, it almost always will be given recognition elsewhere. Thus, if the Massachusetts man's wife had appeared personally in the Florida proceeding or had been represented by an attorney, instead of ignoring it, she would not be allowed to claim later that Florida had no jurisdiction to grant the divorce. Because she would already have had an opportunity to question Florida's right to decree a divorce, she would not be given another day in court to relitigate the same matter; Florida's determination that domicile existed would be *res judicata,* that is, it would be final for those who participated in the suit. In theory, Massachusetts itself might not be bound by the finding, because it was not a party to the Florida action; thus if it wanted to, it might conceivably charge the parties with bigamy if they remarried. In practice, however, this almost never happens; when both spouses participate in the out-of-state action, their divorce is effective.

The key to the validity of a migratory divorce thus turns on whether both parties went along with it. If they did, no one has standing to contest the jurisdictional issue, even if the existence of domicile is shaky, as often is the case. A person who wants an enforceable Nevada divorce must therefore persuade his or her spouse to participate in the proceeding. That spouse need not appear there personally, but must at least be represented by a lawyer. It often takes some negotiation to get a spouse to consent to the divorce. Just as in bargaining for an uncontested cruelty divorce at home, the spouse who desperately wants to end the marriage often must make major concessions in alimony and child custody. The trip to Nevada is sometimes thrown in as part of the deal. As one woman at a Reno ranch said about her husband, "He admitted everything including adultery — why shouldn't he pay extra for riding?"

A few states strongly object to the idea of a husband and wife working out a private arrangement to subvert the restrictions on divorce. Their courts have sometimes permitted relitigation of the domicile question when the basic issue is "matrimonial," that is, when one of the parties decides later that he or she does not want the divorce to be recognized after all; but such states do refuse to open the matter if it is only a "private" controversy, that is, one involving questions of property division. This attempt to protect the home state's interest in preserving marriage has led to a series of decisions which are baroque in their intricacy. Homer Clark has written, "The New York courts, with an ingenuity which would be praiseworthy if employed in a socially useful cause, have succeeded in constructing upon this ostensibly simple distinction, an edifice of inconsistency and confusion unsurpassed elsewhere in the law. Unfortunately for the rest of the nation, their decisions have had some influence in other states."

Migratory divorce is usually associated with situations where one of the spouses goes to another state for a short time, gets a divorce, then comes home. It can also occur, however, when a man remains in the new state, for example Nevada, after getting a divorce. If all his ties to his home state are severed and his stay is long enough, even the most conservative courts will eventually recognize the establishment of domicile and the resulting validity of his divorce. But if the wife did not participate in the proceeding, she may still be able to apply for support, as a wife, or challenge custody in the courts of her home state. This is called "divisible" divorce; the Nevada divorce terminates the marital status, but it does not settle other matters. Finally, as mentioned in

Chapter Five, courts deciding questions of custody often choose to ignore the full faith and credit clause, making their own determinations regardless of what another court may have ordered. A parent who has lost custody in one state consequently may try to kidnap his or her own children in order to retry the issue in the courts of another state.

The foregoing is a vastly simplified introduction to the legal principles that govern migratory divorce. Obviously a lawyer who can unravel the complexities of interstate divorce law and its implications for the validity of decrees, alimony, and custody is well worth his keep. If the husband and wife have agreed to divorce and both have participated in the court action, matters, of course, are greatly simplified.

Through the years different places have been active divorce mills. At the turn of the century, South Dakota and Illinois were popular. In the nineteen-thirties there was hot competition between Arkansas and Nevada for the divorce business, with each state reducing its residency requirement to try to undercut the other. Arkansas was left with a three-month period, while Nevada, not to be undersold, went to six weeks. Chattanooga, Tennessee, was a notorious divorce mill in the nineteen-forties. A judge there set a local record by granting twelve divorces in seventeen minutes. One twenty-seven-year-old woman was divorced there sixteen times. Because Alabama has no minimum waiting period for uncontested cases, it once was a popular refuge for citizens of strict divorce states. During the nineteen-sixties, however, state officials cracked down on local judges who were not requiring substantial proof of domicile. State and federal grand juries indicted some Alabama judges and lawyers for fraud. Other states have uniformly refused to recognize the Alabama quickie divorces as valid; hence that state is no longer the divorce mecca it once was.

Idaho, like Nevada, requires only a six-week residency for divorce; but Sun Valley is not trying to lure any divorce business away from the neighboring state. Everett Taylor, a Sun Valley lawyer, says, "We don't want this to become a divorce mill like Reno. We want only the carriage trade, not the bus trade." Idaho has certainly been attracting the carriage trade— Patricia Kennedy Lawford, Charlotte Ford Niarchos, and the present Mrs. Nelson

Rockefeller all received divorces there. To those who can afford it, six weeks of skiing at Sun Valley or the other resorts is a lot more attractive than spending the same amount of time on a lazy ranch in the Nevada desert.

Reno still continues to be synonymous with easy divorce, and with good reason. Judge Bowen figures that in his twenty years on the bench he has granted roughly eighteen thousand divorces; on busy days he used to hear as many as forty cases. Years ago celebrities like Clark Gable, Mary Pickford, Rita Hayworth, and scores of others gave Reno the publicity that attracted thousands of average people who similarly wanted to end their marriages. Many regarded the trip as an ordeal, penance to be served for having failed at marriage, but for some others it may have been therapeutic. Boston lawyer Norman von Rosenvinge states, "It's good for some people, particularly for a woman who is young enough to feel that her romance has died along with the marriage. Six weeks in another atmosphere, meeting people in the same boat, can help a person adjust to the idea of being divorced. When they come back, they're ready to start things anew."

Although Reno and to a lesser extent Las Vegas still have the reputations of being divorce mills, business is not nearly what it once was. The new California statute and liberalized laws elsewhere may prove to be the death blows to the divorce economy, but the decline actually started before they were enacted. Paul Sorensen, a Las Vegas attorney, thinks the tide turned in the mid-sixties, "primarily because of the quick divorce laws in Mexico." People who had been willing to stay in Reno for six weeks, if that was the only way to get a divorce, flocked to the Mexican border city Juarez, where the whole operation took less than a day.

In 1966 the Nevada legislature tried to compete with Mexico by adding incompatibility as a ground and reducing the separation period from three years to one; the measure was signed by Governor Paul Laxalt, a Catholic, who had previously stated that he would not impose his personal views on others. The new law, however, made little difference, because the cruelty ground had already been broadly applied. People who were willing to incur the cost of going to Nevada and staying there for six weeks were not likely to care whether or not they had to go through the charade of alleging fault to get a divorce.

After the passage of the California law, it became all the more apparent that a more radical change was needed to salvage the dying divorce trade. Howard McKissick, Jr., as Speaker of the Assembly, led a drive to reduce the residency period from six to three weeks. He felt that the availability of one-day Mexican divorce made any talk about the need for a "cooling-off" period irrelevant; people who wanted quick divorces were already getting them. The divorce bar was solidly behind the proposal — there was even talk of cutting the period down to one day — but in spite of claims that the bill would add forty million dollars a year to the Nevada economy, the rest of the community was unenthusiastic. Resort and casino operators realized that the number of divorces would have to double just to compensate for cutting the residency period in half. Jud Allen, then president of Reno's Chamber of Commerce, expressed another common misgiving. "It's not that we wanted to lose the divorce economy, but rather we didn't want that image to hurt our expansion of tourism in other directions." In the past, the Catholic Church had tolerated the liberal divorce laws, but this time it spoke up to oppose loosening them still further. Many people apparently were uneasy about the idea of a husband and wife, who had sat down together for a Thanksgiving dinner, being able to get divorced and remarried before Christmas.

In spite of the opposition, the proposal was passed by the Nevada Assembly and came within a single vote of being approved in the Senate. According to McKissick, he had thought he had enough votes for passage, but one senator who had promised to vote "yes" showed up dead drunk and mistakenly voted "no." As a result, the six-week residency period still stands, and the present number of divorces granted in Nevada is a fraction of what it was twenty years ago. Yet Reno seems to be prospering; only the legal profession has felt the decline. McKissick says that "lawyers are dropping like flies." He once handled one hundred and fifty divorces a year at three hundred and fifty dollars apiece, but now his total has been cut in half. He has been able to make up the slack with other kinds of legal work, but thinks that there are older lawyers who "don't know how to do anything else."

Not everyone paints such a dismal picture. Prince Hawkins, the chairman of the Economics Committee of the Nevada Bar Association, says that "divorce was never a major part of many attorneys' practices; the change has been gradual and people have adjusted to it." He sees no need for reducing the waiting period; in fact, he seems happy to see the divorce business decline as "it is bad for our image." Legal practice in Nevada now largely resembles that in any other state. McKissick, however, is still disappointed that his proposal was not accepted. When it was defeated, he said, "Nevada will have its alleged image, but Mexico will have all the money."

During the nineteen-sixties Mexico became a much more popular place to get a divorce than Nevada. Precise figures are not available, but it has been estimated that during that period anywhere from ten to thirty thousand New Yorkers a year ended their marriages in Mexico. In comparison the total number of divorces in Nevada in 1969 was roughly ten thousand, and that figure included people from every state. The easy residency requirements of some Mexican states made divorce there particularly attractive. It was not even necessary to stay overnight in order to become a resident and get a divorce; one simply had to register at the local city hall and one was a resident. Indeed, as far as Mexican authorities were concerned, the whole operation could be done by mail.

In many states, the validity of Mexican divorces was hazy at best. Residence in Juarez was only fleeting, and, in most cases, there was not the slightest evidence of domicile. Moreover, even if residence and domicile were somehow more convincing, the Constitution does not require a state to give full faith and credit to judgments of foreign countries, though the doctrine of comity requires that they be given at least a gesture of respect. In 1948 New York's highest court refused to recognize Mexican mail-order divorces in which neither spouse had ever appeared there personally. Because such divorces were cheap and required no waiting period, the courts of most states regarded them as a much more serious threat than Reno divorces to their restrictive laws. Similarly, most American courts invalidated unilateral Mexican divorces, that is, divorces in which only one spouse had participated.

New Jersey and a few other conservative states also held that all quickie Mexican divorces were invalid, no matter who had participated or appeared. In most others, however, including New York, it remained open whether a Mexican divorce might be valid if one spouse had gone there and the other had at least been represented by an attorney. Although not constitutionally compelled to do so, the New York court decided in 1965 that if both parties had submitted to Mexican jurisdiction, their divorce was valid. The court reasoned that it would be inconsistent to uphold Nevada divorces, yet deny Mexican ones; in both instances, residency and particularly domicile were really shams, and there was no substantial difference between six weeks and one day. Moreover, the court indicated that a person who has gone along with an out-of-state divorce and accepted the benefits of it should not later be allowed to contest its validity. The decision caused tens of thousands of New Yorkers to heave a collective sigh of relief and it created a boom for Juarez. Celebrities received the publicity, but average people made up the bulk of the trade. A flight to El Paso, a trip across the Rio Grande to Juarez, and a flight home the next day were within the means of many people.

The sudden availability of easy divorce was one of the principal reasons why reform became palatable to conservatives in New York. In accepting a general liberalization of the law, however, they insisted on a provision that was an attempt to curb migratory divorce. It provided that a person who obtained an out-of-state divorce and returned to New York within eighteen months would be presumed to have been domiciled in New York for the entire time; unless there was strong evidence to rebut this presumption of New York domicile, the out-of-state divorce would be invalid. The language of the provision was ambiguous and there was some doubt about both its constitutionality and its applicability to foreign divorces, but it panicked many New Yorkers into believing that Mexican divorces would no longer be available. Kenneth Kaplan, a New York lawyer, explained at the time that it was not at all clear whether the provision would invalidate future quickie divorces. "A valid case can be made for both views. But for a divorce client sitting in a lawyer's office, that has all the comfort of being told the glass of water he or she is about to drink may be poisoned or may not be." The new law was also going to broaden the grounds for divorce in New York, but many people apparently did not like the idea of having either to allege cruelty or wait out a two-year separation period in order to get a decree. In the last month before the new law went into effect, more than eight thousand New York couples got divorces in Juarez. On the final day, one thousand divorces were granted and thousands of people were still shut out. For a time New York's ambiguous jurisdictional provision intimidated its citizens from going to Mexico for divorce, but eventually most of the business returned; ultimately the antimigratory divorce provision was repealed.

The local government in Juarez and other Mexican communities which specialized in the divorce trade were delighted with the money it brought in, but the national government did not like the image it gave the country. At one point Frank Sinatra was banned from Mexico for making cutting remarks about its divorce practices in a movie, Second Honeymoon. In late 1970 new laws went into effect in Mexico which required a residency period of several months, as well as the appearance of both parents and all children in court for the hearing. Lawyers in Juarez hoped they would find a way around the regulations, but they have had little success; hence quickie divorce is dead in Mexico.

Not every country, however, is inclined to put its reputation ahead of its income. Two countries on the Caribbean island of Hispanola, Haiti and the Dominican Republic, quickly jumped into the vacuum Mexico had left. Both were careful to pattern their laws after the old Mexican statute in the hope that if New York and other states had upheld Mexican divorces, they would also uphold Caribbean dissolutions. The cost of a Caribbean divorce varies from three to five hundred dollars, not counting travel, lodging, and American legal fees. The governments, or people close to them, get most of the basic fee. Just as mercenaries at the end of one war seem to congregate at the next potential trouble spot, divorce lawyers from Alabama and Mexico have found their way to Hispanola. In Santo Domingo, Manuel Espinosa, a veteran of Juarez, helps coordinate the Dominican divorces; and Alabamian Donald McKay does the same thing in Port-au-Prince, Haiti. He says, "We'll divorce 'em in the morning, and, if they want, marry 'em in the afternoon."

Patronage by movie stars like Elliot Gould and Jane Fonda has helped publicize Caribbean divorce, but thus far business has not come close to matching Mexico's heyday. Some people are scared away by the banana republic image that both countries share. Also because Caribbean divorces are not yet well known, people may be skeptical about their validity. Many lawyers assume that because the laws so closely parallel the former Mexican statute, they must be valid; in many states they are. One lawyer, however, cautions any male client he has to send his wife to the Caribbean, rather than go himself. "Then she will never be able to contest it. If she does not go, even if she agrees to the divorce at this time, conceivably she may contest it at some future time by claiming fraud, forgery, or any one of a number of things. It is unlikely anything like this will happen, of course, but it is always possible. Much better for you to sign the papers and let her make the trip. Then there's no possibility she can contest it."

This tactic may prevent a spouse from ever challenging the validity of the divorce, but it does not necessarily mean that the divorce is ironclad. In 1972 a lower New Jersey court in effect ruled that Haitian divorces are invalid in that state (as were Mexican divorces). Interestingly, the suit was not brought by a husband or wife trying to fight a divorce. Instead it was started by the Attorney General's office against a company which sold a package tour that included a round-trip flight to Haiti, a hotel for two days, and a divorce for about twelve hundred dollars. The court issued a permanent injunction against the sale of the tours on the ground that since the divorces were invalid, the trips were worthless; hence their marketing violated New Jersey's consumer protection statute. The company appealed the injunction, but in the meantime moved to New York where it hoped for more hospitable treatment; since then, the New York courts have upheld Caribbean divorce.

Migratory divorce has existed for almost a century. Until the laws of all states are uniformly liberal, it will be with us at least to an extent in the future; a few states and countries will always be willing to cater to the demand for quick divorce. Some social planners have advocated setting aside certain portions of a community for gambling, prostitution, and other unseemly activities; and in a sense, we seem to have done the same thing on a national scale for divorce. Without discussing the merit of the proposal for other activities, it is not appropriate for divorce. Massachusetts may decide that it has a particularly strong commitment to family stability, but that policy is not served by forcing its citizens who wish to divorce to conduct their ugly business in Reno. It is not the legal formality of divorce which is troublesome; it is the after-effects. Migratory divorce spares Massachusetts only the embarrassment of statistics — the divorce is recorded in Reno, not Boston — but Massachusetts, not Nevada, must cope with the problems created by the broken family.

The availability of out-of-state divorce tends to undermine the laws of a conservative state like Massachusetts. Those people who can afford a short trip — and more and more can — easily get around the supposedly restrictive laws. Attempts to prevent migratory divorce have largely been futile. There have been some vague opinions by the A.B.A.'s Committee on Professional Ethics which indicate that a lawyer who advises his client to go out of the country for a divorce may be subject to disciplinary action. Massachusetts has a statute which purports to make it a crime for a lawyer to send his clients out of state to get divorces. Those few Massachusetts lawyers who are aware of the law regard it as a joke; yet it remains on the books. Nevertheless, Homer Clark has warned, "The law in this area is in such a state of hypocrisy and dishonesty that a lawyer who gives realistic advice about migratory divorce places his professional reputation at some hazard."

As divorce laws are steadily being liberalized, the incidence of migratory divorce is slowly diminishing; and the states which once prospered from it are being forced to turn to other enterprises. Ironically, Nevada is turning toward the marriage industry. In spite of its divorce mill reputation, Reno may now be the marriage capital of the country. In 1969 there were more than eight marriages for every one divorce in Nevada, a ratio that is more than double that of most states. Just as Nevada once specialized in easy divorce, it is now exploiting easy marriage. No blood tests are required and there is no waiting period; it takes about ten minutes to get a license and go through a ceremony.

Until recently, the marriage business meant six-figure incomes to Nevada justices of the peace, who collected a fee for each service they performed; but, now that business has really taken off, it has been given to salaried marriage commissioners, and the state reaps the profits. The people who marry in Nevada usually spend their honeymoon there as well, not for six weeks certainly, but long enough to give considerable business to hotels, restaurants, and casinos. Most of the newlyweds come from states where blood tests and waiting periods mean unwanted delay. Those who marry on impulse and refuse to wait a few days are the very people who are particularly likely to divorce later. Nevada has thus reversed the cycle. Californians now go to Reno for easy marriage, but then when it does not work out, they stay home to get divorced.

# Chapter Ten

# Till Divorce Do Us Part

Some people think the most effective way of solving the problem of divorce in our society is to reform our marriage laws. In 1971 and again in 1972, Lena Lee, a member of the Maryland House of Delegates, introduced a bill to create three-year, renewable "contract marriages." According to her plan, an engaged couple would work out a marriage contract, then sign it on their wedding day. The contract would automatically terminate three years later unless both parties elected to renew it. In effect, a couple could dissolve their marriage without interference by the state. If either person wanted to end the marriage, that is, not renew the contract, his or her spouse would have no power to continue it, though he or she could go to court to settle any property and custody disputes.

The proposal has never gotten out of committee, but its novelty has already attracted a great deal of national attention, much of it critical, most of the rest humorous. The idea of a marriage automatically expiring, much like a dog license, disturbs those people who believe that "till death do us part" must be the foundation of any marriage vow. Yet our vows are already out of line with reality. No matter how optimistic and loving a person may feel on his or her wedding day, he or she knows, if only subconsciously, that divorce is available should the marriage turn sour. We may extol the ideal of lifelong relationships, but the prevalance of divorce today is bound to bring our own aspirations a little closer to earth.

The idea of trial marriage cuts harshly against the grain of our cultural heritage. To many people it suggests loose living and irresponsibility. It may seem to betray a certain weakness of character to want to strike the words "sickness" and "bad times" from the marriage ceremony. Perhaps at the core, the concept of trial marriage challenges the principle that people would have just one sex partner during life. Although these kinds of attitudes may be basic to many people's conception of marriage, they have little relation to that institution as it actually exists. The alternative of divorce, even if it is economically and emotionally expensive, already makes every union a trial marriage.

Moreover, we do not need sociologists to tell us that it is increasingly acceptable for couples to live together and even have children without the benefit of clergy. It is inconsistent to oppose legitimizing trial marriages when they are already practiced with little penalty. There can be times, of course, when it is wise to be inconsistent, to overlook reality in favor of supporting a higher ideal, even if it is unattainable. Arguably, if our laws did not purport to create marriage as a lifelong relationship, if we aimed for less, we would have even more disruption of family stability than we do now. Because this kind of argument is abstract, it is hard to rebut on any but its own terms. On balance, it seems to this writer more sensible to deal with marriage as it really is than with an ideal that fewer and fewer people seem to respect. Instead of elevating marriage, a supposedly restrictive divorce law degrades it if it is blatantly flouted. We now rely on divorce and desertion to serve people's need for flexibility, but we might win more respect for marriage by making it conform more closely to actual social behavior.

The idea of legislating trial marriage is new, so there has been little public debate about how the details might be worked out. For instance, should it be based on a specified period, like the three years in the Lee plan, or should a trial marriage be terminable at any time by either party? Setting a minimum time limit would discourage frivolous trial marriages, though people certainly could separate before the time expired. Some may feel a three-year period is too long, but for the experience to be a true test of mutual commitment, there must be considerably more at stake than in a casual affair. At the same time, if trial marriage were to be effective, it would have to ensure that a person who did not want to continue the marriage would be able to get out painlessly. The decision to go ahead with the relationship should be thought of as a positive step, not the product of momentum. A couple who, at the end of the three-year period, decided to extend their marriage should perhaps have to manifest publicly their renewed commitment to one another in some sort of ceremony, while those who do not want to continue together should be able to dissolve their marriage as inconspicuously as possible. It would also have to be decided whether people who did want to extend their marriage would simply sign on for another three-year hitch, or would enter into a conventional marital relationship.

Margaret Mead has advocated the creation of two kinds of marriage, but she draws the line between them in a somewhat different way. "We badly need to recognize a new form of marriage — a marriage between childless partners with no commitment to continuity. Such marriages should be easier to contract, should involve no automatic economic relationships, and should be capable of dissolution by mutual consent, without undue delay, cost, or supervision from the constituted organs of society. On the other hand, marriages which are parental should be placed in a different category, and have built into them once more the conception of what marriage with children is — a lifelong relationship which will end only with death."

It is logical to distinguish between childless and parental marriages as they involve quite different expectations and obligations, not just by the particular husbands and wives, but by society as a whole. Much of the concern voiced about divorce is related to its effect on children; where there are none, the argument for state regulation of marriage is far weaker. The Mead proposal might encourage some people to think more carefully about what they really wanted from marriage and to choose accordingly. The prospect of a lifelong commitment might not be so attractive if a socially acceptable alternative were available.

In spite of its theoretical appeal, however, the Mead proposal is probably unworkable. Many marriages are the result of pregnancy, and this is particularly the case with younger couples. Estimates vary somewhat, but perhaps as many as half the women who marry before age twenty are pregnant at the time. Some of these pregnancies are planned in order to get parents to go along with an early marriage, others occur after the engagement is announced, but apparently most are accidental. The President's Commission on Population Growth and the American Future reported that forty-six percent of American women now have sexual intercourse in their teens, and most of them do not use contraceptives. Many happen to get pregnant and hence want to marry. To lock women in such circumstances into a "lifelong commitment" at such an early age would seem to defeat Mrs. Mead's purpose. The specter of a law that prevents people with children from ever divorcing might deter some unwanted pregnancies, but doubtlessly many would still occur. The only solution consistent with the spirit of her proposal would be to discourage young marriage even if pregnancy is involved. This would take a reversal of the common belief that marriage is the "right" thing in such situations. It is also not clear what course of action would be preferable to marriage. For many people abortion is morally unacceptable, yet women who are deemed too young to marry may also be too young to raise children on their own. Putting children up for adoption might be best for some people, but that solution could not be forced on everyone.

Also, it is not clear whether Mead intended to imply by her phrase "a lifelong relationship which will end only in death" that divorce would never be open to a couple once they had children. Should such a ban apply after the children are adult? When the children leave home a marriage can be severely tested, and, if it unfortunately fails the test, there seems to be little purpose in denying divorce. Moreover, there are certainly instances where divorce is preferable to marriage even though there are minor children in the family. It is doubtful that Margaret Mead or many other people would want to deny a divorce to Eva McNulty, the woman described in Chapter One whose husband was convicted and jailed for committing incest with their thirteen-year-old daughter. Some allowance would have to be made for cases of such serious hardship, but doing so would undermine much of the utility of the two-marriage scheme, because it would blur the distinctions between them.

The unfortunate weakness of the Mead plan is that it depends on people's making careful, reasoned choices about their lives.

One does not have to be a cynic to believe that marriage and children are not always the products of deliberate choice. This human failing might be tempered if the choices and their ramifications were made clearer, but it cannot be completely eradicated. Couples who now try to salvage shaky marriages by having children might act differently if they knew that act would foreclose divorce. But until there are sweeping educational and moral changes, it seems unlikely it would have much of an effect on younger people, and young marriages are those that are most divorce prone. As discussed in Chapter Five, the same standard for divorce should apply whether or not there are children; but it may be wise to employ different procedures, so that if counseling services are limited, they can be concentrated on families with children.

Instead of legislating new forms of marriage, people might be allowed to make their own contracts before marrying; these might provide for the possibility of divorce, though such provisions are not judicially enforceable under present law. Even if marriage contracts were made fully enforceable, the greatest benefit they offer might be indirect. A couple that takes the job of drafting such a contract seriously — and not everyone would — must carefully define each person's rights and responsibilities. Conflicts which might have remained latent may be identified early enough to allow resolution; after a marriage has started to deteriorate, it may be too late.

Because changing the basic structure of marriage is such a monumental undertaking, some people believe that the most realistic way to attack the problem of divorce is to make it more difficult to marry, either by raising the minimum age or by requiring a longer waiting period. Various studies indicate that a man who marries when he is in his teens is two or three times more likely to divorce than one who marries in his twenties. Estimates of the exact odds vary, but sociologist John Scanzoni states, "Clearly, to be married at a young age is to be at extraordinarily high risk in terms of marital dissolution."

Most people commonly ascribe the connection between young marriage and higher risk of divorce to immaturity. Brooks Potter says, "Young people today will make a more careful investigation of a second-hand car they're thinking of buying than of the person they are going to marry." Long engagements are decidedly out of fashion, and the average marital age has apparently been going down for some time. Many people see a simple solution: raise the minimum marrying age.

Interestingly enough, the Uniform Marriage and Divorce Act has done just the opposite, establishing eighteen as the minimum marrying age for men and women who lack parental consent, and sixteen for those with either the consent of their parents or the approval of a judge. Judge Ralph Podell, the former chairman of the Family Law Section of the A.B.A., says his own experiences on the bench have made him "bitterly opposed" to these provisions. "Nothing hurts me more than the two weeks each year that I have to serve as duty judge and act as 'parson' part of the time. On a Friday, it's nothing to marry twenty-five couples, and it gets depressing to see eighteen-year-olds, both in school, not working, come in to get married. Half the time the parents don't know anything about it." The thought of having to officiate at marriages of people sixteen or even younger makes his blood boil. "The Uniform Act provides that a judge shall approve a license for a person under sixteen years old if it's in his best interest and if he is 'capable of assuming the responsibilities of marriage.' Forgive my language, but who the hell under age sixteen understands the 'responsibilities of marriage' or is capable of handling them?" The drafters of the act stress that in such cases the court should make a careful determination of an underage applicant's best interests, and that pregnancy alone does not establish that it is best for a young person to marry. Judge Podell, however, is not alone in doubting the act's wisdom in this regard. Several of the states that have patterned their laws after the Uniform Act have eliminated the provisions regulating marriage.

At the heart of the act's marital age provisions is a sense that because people are now granted the right to vote and drink at eighteen (and if the draft is reestablished, the duty to fight), it would be inconsistent and perhaps unfair to set a higher age for marriage. A good argument can be made that it takes different kinds of traits and skills to vote than to marry, but there is an appealing simplicity in having one sharp line separating minority and adulthood. More important, a higher age would only increase the problem of premarital pregnancy. It would be a mistake, for instance, to forbid all people under age twenty-one to marry, regardless of pregnancy; but it would be equally dangerous to make a general prohibition and then to create pregnancy as an exception to the rule. Underage couples who wanted to marry would be strongly tempted to qualify for the exception. The relatively low age set by the act also reflects the fact that such limits have been loosely applied in the past. Representative Robert Drinan has commented that it is "surely ironic that many states enforce their legal ban on alcohol to minors much more stringently than they do their laws prohibiting marriage without parental consent to young persons under a certain age."

Whether we are smitten with the idea of young love or it is simply too costly to enforce the restrictions, minimum age requirements have not been successful in deterring youthful marriage. Such requirements, even if more consistently applied, probably deal more with symptoms than causes. Immaturity is certainly one reason why early marriage is risky, but there are others. People in their teens earn far less money than do those in their twenties, they tend to have less education, they are more likely to be burdened with the responsibility of children early in marriage, and they are, of course, married somewhat longer than people who wed later in life. That young people find marriage more trying than do their older counterparts may not reveal weakness of character and judgment on their parts, so much as it reflects the fact that they must face much harsher circumstances. To some extent, the answer may be not blanket prohibition against young marriage but an effort to ameliorate the particular problems which go with it. To give just one example, if child care centers were made available to those who desired them, a young husband and wife would have a greater chance for the economic stability so important to a healthy marriage. In being preoccupied with age alone, we may not be addressing the underlying reasons for marital disruption.

It also has been proposed that marrying be made harder by imposing a longer waiting period between the time of application for a marriage license and the time it becomes effective. The Uniform Act provides for a three-day period, which is consistent with the present laws of most states. Three days is long enough to deter on-the-spot marriages and precludes hasty action even over long weekends. The drafters of the act felt a longer period would not effectively discourage other potentially risky marriages, in the belief that once a person has gone so far as to register his or her name with a government official, it may be hard for that person to back out. Longer waiting periods have not really been given a fair test, however, as judges have frequently exercised their power to waive them, and there have always been states like Georgia and Nevada which cater to the demand for quickie marriage. If somehow a universal thirty-day rule were adopted, some people, who otherwise would have gone through with an ill-conceived marriage, might change their minds. Even though relatively few people would do so, the gain would be achieved at little cost. It is not a hardship to require people who wish to legalize an ostensibly lifelong relationship to make their arrangements one month in advance.

There is growing support for making the process of marrying, if not more difficult, at least more thoughtful by requiring couples to participate in premarital counseling before receiving a marriage license. California took a step in this direction in 1970 by enacting a statute requiring all persons under eighteen to apply to the superior court for permission to marry. The new law further requires that such people participate in marriage counseling, and though the court is given power to waive this requirement, it seldom does so. Underage applicants are singled out for counseling because of their particularly high divorce rate. The program has had only a mixed success, but it is probably too soon to make a conclusive evaluation. Some California courts do have marriage counselors on their staffs because of their conciliation programs, but the extra workload imposed by the new statute has required that most applicants be referred to either clergymen or outside agencies. The statute itself does not define the kind of counseling which should be given, and, though some courts have issued guidelines, experiences vary from case to case.

The biggest obstacle encountered by the program has been public hostility. Judge William Hogoboom has noted that this was a particular problem when the law first went into effect, because few people had heard of it. "When, as was not uncommon, they arrived on Friday (after school) for a license, and the invitations, the church, minister, caterer, attendants, rented fineries, cake, and all the other logistic accompaniments to a well-run wedding were scheduled for Saturday, the cries of anguish over a delay of a week or two for counseling took on the magnitude and ferocity of a hurricane. With some justification, parents thought this judicial (really legislative) interference with their filial [sic] duties amounted to unbearable governmental officiousness."

Even now when the requirement is better known, people still do not apply for a license until they have made up their minds to marry. Because the counselors become involved very late in the process, their function is limited. This constraint has been compounded by the fact that fifty percent of the couples who have been counseled involve pregnancies, and a large majority of the couples who apply already have the approval of their parents to marry. As a result, the courts have turned down only three percent of the marriage applications they have received from underage people. Judge Hogoboom says that he sees nothing in this rate that "would indicate that this law will stem the tide of dissolution among youthful marriages. It is doubtful that it will even cause a ripple in the current." He does see some positive signs, however, which he believes justify continuing the program. "One important by-product is to make young people aware that there is a source of assistance in the community should difficulties arise later in their marriage."

The history of a much smaller premarital counseling program in Iowa indicates this hope may unfortunately be unfounded. A follow-up study there showed that in three years not one person had returned to the counseling agency, although it was known that some of the couples were in need of help. The Iowa program was unable either to discourage early marriages or to encourage later reliance on counseling services — if anything it made people antagonistic toward them — so it was discontinued. One counselor who was involved in the program believes that any new effort must reach people before they come to the decision to marry, and that their participation must be voluntary. Unless both these conditions are observed, premarital counseling is likely to create self-defeating hostility. For such counseling to achieve its purpose, it would have to be conducted on a scale and with an intensity that has not yet been attempted. Up till now, it has generally been limited to underage people, and it has done little to discourage risky marriages. Whether it has helped make such marriages a little less risky is not known. One type of premarital counseling that deserves greater consideration is legal counseling; before they wed, people should learn how marriage will affect their legal rights and responsibilities, in regard to income, property, and choice of domicile.

In time our laws governing marriage may change, but patterns of social behavior will probably have to change first. No state has come close to legalizing trial marriages, though they already exist outside the law. Eventually our formal institutions may have to be adjusted to conform more closely to our practices. In respect at least to marriage, the law follows behavior, if slowly, rather than the other way around. Homer Clark has noted that some statutes, such as traffic or antitrust laws, function not only to provide rules in the event of litigation, but also to regulate social conduct. "This is not true of the divorce laws, however. They generally have little impact on the conduct of married persons who, in our society and perhaps in other societies, work out their style of living together with virtually no attention to the law's prescriptions." We are living in a period of such rapid social change that it is impossible to predict just how our institutions will evolve. Any reform of marriage and divorce laws must then reflect our present needs and values; if those change in unforeseen ways, then another reform will have to be undertaken.

The fundamental difficulty with our traditional divorce laws is that they do not reflect the realities of contemporary marriage. Still based on the notion that marriages are made in heaven, they presume that marriage problems must be the product of human fault. We have become lax in our regulation of marriage, but we have retained the trappings of being strict in respect to divorce. Margaret Mead has stated that "we insist that the most flimsy, ill-conceived, and unsuitable mating be treated as a sanctified, lifelong choice. At the same time, we insist that every divorce, however much it is dictated by every consideration of the welfare of the children and parents, be regarded as a failure and be listed as an index of social disorder — along with suicide, homicide, narcotic addiction, alcoholism, and crime."

Those who favor retaining fault-based divorce argue that it reflects society's interest in family stability. Although it is easy to sympathize with the motive, it is hard to agree with the means.

If we are truly interested in preserving families, we must act long before divorce is sought, for at that point there may be very little left to rescue. The imposition of strict divorce laws gives the false assurance that marriages are being preserved when, in many instances, only the legal status remains. Instead of being preoccupied with making the process of getting a divorce difficult, we should be exploring means of making divorce less necessary and, where such efforts fail, making divorce less of a hardship on all those involved.

It has also been suggested that our present system is the best of both worlds: we have strict laws on the books that symbolize our ideal of marriage as a lifelong relationship through thick and thin, but we also provide in practice devices like collusion and migratory divorce to mitigate any harshness of the written law. This suggestion ignores several important points. First, fault-based divorce carries with it certain innate evils. It forces the accusation of wrongdoing, thereby diverting attention from the real problems of a marriage. The legal name-calling is bound to contribute to the hostility between the spouses. There are some experienced family lawyers, however, who contend that hostility is inherent in divorce, and there is nothing the law can do to lessen it. In some instances this may be true. In divorce disputes the battle itself is often more important than the booty. One Michigan couple was able to work out a division of financial assets and real estate but could not agree on how to divide the groceries in the pantry; neither spouse was willing to concede to the other that extra box of corn flakes, so they went to court to settle it.

George Snyder, a Detroit lawyer, says, "If there was one strength of the fault system it was that it required a person to sit down in a lawyer's office and say, 'This is what my spouse did to me.' I've talked with behavioral scientists who feel that the divorce process should be therapeutic, that people should have an outlet to get their aggressions out in a socially acceptable way. Fighting over pots and pans can sound bad, but it's a lot better than having people knocked around or beaten up."

One can agree with Snyder's conclusion that divorces are naturally bitter, however, without concurring with his judgment that the fault system is therapeutic. As Homer Clark has stated, "If the hostility is so intense there might be physical violence, then a psychiatrist is called for. Going through the 'cruelty' charade won't vent resentments that run that deep." It is doubtful that the premise of fault-based divorce — that one spouse is presumed to be totally to blame for the breakdown while the other is innocent — can contribute to a healthy resolution of the bitterness that accompanies the death of a marriage. Snyder is probably right when he says that "the idea of 'friendly divorce' isn't often viable," but we should not lose sight of the need to design a divorce process that encourages people to face their real problems, not fictional ones, so that they can better adjust to their post-divorce responsibilities. The enactment of no-fault divorce does not magically make everything friendly, but several years' experience in California and elsewhere has shown that it can make the atmosphere noticeably more civilized.

There are still other shortcomings of fault divorce that have been discussed at some length in the preceding chapters. Fault divorce fosters a dirty kind of bargaining where support and custody of children are traded for the right to end the marriage. The requirement of having to prove certain grounds also leads people to ask whether they *can* get a divorce, rather than whether they *should*. These are substantial prices to pay for maintaining a symbol of ideal marriage. In truth, that symbol is badly tarnished. Far from regarding divorce law as the embodiment of our highest aspirations, most people see it as hypocritical and out of date. Our laws should be reformed to reflect the fact that many people marry young, others marry casually, and still others encounter difficulties that cannot be overcome. The marriages of such people can break down without misconduct on anyone's part.

Some people are genuinely concerned that if the necessity of proving fault is removed from the divorce laws, people will resort to divorce whenever their marriages run into trouble. Congressman Robert Drinan has stated, "Every survey of married couples seems to indicate that in the overwhelming majority of normally successful marriages one or both of the partners felt for a period of time that the marriage was a mistake and could not work. How many married persons act on this conviction and obtain a divorce simply because a quick divorce is practically advertised by the law as a permanent remedy for marital unhappiness?" Drinan thinks that there are already many such people and, if the divorce laws are eased, their number would be considerably increased.

The impression that no-fault divorce would encourage more people to escape their problems by walking out on them is widespread, yet it overlooks several important considerations. Collusion and migratory divorce already make it easy, in a legal sense, for couples to end their marriages. It is only when one spouse balks that the fault system shuts off the escape, and even then desertion is a possibility. There are significant deterrents to divorce that operate outside the laws; social pressures imposed by the expectations of children, family, and friends all work to keep a marriage going. Paul Bohannan states, "I have never known a divorced person who got his divorce for silly or flimsy reasons. The grounds may have been trumped up and absurd — but the reasons were not. Ease and difficulty have little to do with grounds. Rather, they have to do with emotional tension and legal procedures that accompany divorce. Easing the grounds always follows wholesale dishonesty in using the grounds that were previously available — it is the law catching up with the community."

What then of the statistics that show an increase in the number of divorces in most of the states that have enacted no-fault statutes? They clearly show that no-fault has had an impact on people's behavior, still it is not at all evident that it has actually aggravated family instability. Some of the increase is related to a corresponding decrease in migratory divorce. This is all to the good: it serves no purpose — other than to line the pockets of Reno lawyers — for people to have to travel to Nevada to get divorced. Lawyers in California, Vermont, and elsewhere believe that some of the increase is attributable to people now getting divorces who before had resorted to desertion. This is also to the good, as it allows people to establish legitimate second families. Some of the increase is the natural product of population growth, as well.

There are certainly some people who get divorced under no-fault but would have remained married under the previous law, though such cases may be rarer than is generally supposed. For those people who are truly on the edge in deciding whether or not to divorce, the business of having to allege fault and barter to get a spouse not to contest may be enough to swing the balance toward staying married. Elizabeth Selby of Boston went to her lawyer several years ago to see about getting a divorce. "He said that I would have to accuse my husband of cruelty, and neither of us wanted to go through with that, so we've just muddled through. If it had just been a matter of saying that our marriage was dead, I think I would have gone through with the divorce." Mrs. Selby sometimes regrets not having done so. "We have a nice home and a lovely daughter. I'm more or less resigned to the idea that there isn't anything between my husband and me. He has his life and I have mine. I still think about getting out, but I have some friends who are divorced and I know it's not that easy out there either."

It is tempting to come to glib judgments in such cases — to say that society is better off because the Selbys are still married or to say that the laws should not force people to lead emotionally empty lives. In truth, no one, not even the Selbys, knows where they would be if there had been a divorce. It is possible that Elizabeth Selby and her husband and daughter would have been more fulfilled and content; it is also possible that one or all of them might have been miserable. Because no one does really know, because the question is so debatable, the choice to divorce should be the individual's to make for better or worse without having to run a legal obstacle course.

There are a number of ways to eliminate fault from divorce. The simplest and possibly the best is to abolish all the conventional fault grounds and to allow divorce after a reasonable period of separation. Separation is a fairly clear indication of marital discord; few people who want to divorce wish to continue to live together. Aside from requiring unjustifiably long periods of separation, the basic shortcoming of living-apart statutes in the past is that they have often inadvertently discouraged reconciliation by penalizing couples who make honest but ineffective efforts to get back together. Separation must be broadly defined so that people who want to try to work out their problems are not deterred from doing so by being required to wait longer for their divorce should they fail.

The most common approach in the new no-fault statutes has been the marriage-breakdown test under which a person who wants a divorce claims that irreconcilable differences have arisen or that the marriage has become unsupportable. If the breakdown statutes were applied literally, they would represent a step backward from the traditional divorce system. A hearing to determine if the differences were indeed irreconcilable would probe into intimate matters that are better left private. For that matter, the test set by such statutes often seems impossible to meet: who is to say that the marital differences are absolutely irreconcilable? In practice, however, most courts have treated the marriage-breakdown standards as actually being divorce on demand. If a couple — or even one spouse — says that the marriage is dead, that statement is regarded as conclusive and the courts will not rule otherwise. The breakdown test has been a politically acceptable way of adopting divorce by demand, an approach that people are ready to accept in practice, but apparently not in principle. Hypocrisy thus has not been fully purged from the divorce laws, yet under no-fault its effects are not pernicious.

For divorce reform to be fully effective, all fault grounds should be eliminated. As was the case in Texas, tacking a no-fault ground onto an existing divorce statute may be the only feasible way of enacting reform, but the results are not completely satisfactory. Some reformers believe that annulment and legal separation are relics of archaic law and should also be scrapped, but, for Catholics and members of other religious groups, these are the only morally acceptable avenues for terminating marriage, so they should be preserved.

The requirement of proving fault pervades the laws and practices governing the collateral issues of divorce, particularly alimony and child custody. In addition to changing the grounds for divorce, it is necessary to revise the laws relating to marital property to reflect emerging recognition of married women's rights. Marital fault that does not directly bear on a child's relationship to his parents should not be considered in custody disputes; his best interests should control. We should acknowledge that a mother is not necessarily the best custodian for children, but in close cases we must also remember that it would be unfair to generations of women who have been trained only to be housekeepers and mothers to take children from them simply to honor sexual egalitarianism. There should also be some mechanism that ensures that the interests of the children of divorce are adequately presented to the court.

Eliminating marital fault from the grounds for divorce and, where appropriate, from consideration in collateral matters, can solve some but certainly not all the problems of divorce. To the extent that economic difficulties are at the root of much marital instability and exacerbate the problems of divorce, a much broader response is necessary. Extensive social reorganization may be needed. On a less ambitious scale, we must develop effective ways of helping families that are in trouble. When it comes to providing family services, too many state legislators have been generous with platitudes, but niggardly with tangible resources. Intensive counseling may not be possible, but there should be at least some sort of conciliation service that gives people who have asked for divorce a way out if they change their minds. This is especially important if no-fault statutes are to be applied so that divorce can be had by demand.

No-fault divorce is not entirely new; some states have had no-fault grounds for over a hundred years, although they have not been extensively used until now. Only in the last several years have such states as California, Iowa, Florida, and a handful of others totally abolished the traditional fault grounds, such as adultery and cruelty. It would be premature to pronounce a final word on the impact of the new no-fault laws, though, in those states which have enacted them, the response of judges, lawyers, and, most important, people getting divorce, has been almost uniformly favorable. We need to define the issues more clearly; we need to identify the constituencies for and against reform; and we must honestly admit what we do and do not know about divorce. Only by sweeping away the myths and clichés which have distorted much of the debate about divorce reform can we equip ourselves to make intelligent and humane judgments about a complex and poorly understood issue.

# Suggestions for Further Reading

I hope that this book illuminates the background of the movement for no-fault divorce, as well as the issues that it raises; but nothing written at this time can presume to pronounce the final word on its impact. For those who want to read more about divorce law, particularly traditional practices, I recommend three books which were most useful to me:

Bohannan, Paul (ed.), *Divorce and After* (New York: Doubleday, 1970).

Clark, Homer H., Jr., *The Law of Domestic Relations in the United States* (St. Paul, Minn.: West Publishing Company, 1968).

Rheinstein, Max, *Marriage Stability, Divorce, and the Law* (Chicago: The University of Chicago Press, 1972).

The articles in the Bohannan collection are primarily concerned with the psychological and sociological aspects of divorce; Clark's book is essentially an encyclopedia of American domestic relations law; and Rheinstein's perspective is historical and cultural. All three books are copiously footnoted, thus they provide an entry into the scholarly literature on divorce.

Divorce reform is taking place so rapidly, much of what was written only a few years ago is already somewhat dated. Many law reviews have published articles on new and proposed statutes. (Law reviews are well-indexed and are generally available in law school libraries and some courthouses and bar associations.) The *Journal of Family Law* and the *Family Law Quarterly* are devoted solely to the law of domestic relations; the latter is published by the American Bar Association, but its editors present a wide range of opinions.

# Index

Fathers United for Equal Rights: 136, 138

Fault: evidence of in no-fault proceeding, 25, 33; problem in assigning, 12

Feminists: and alimony, 53, 139; reform effort, 139–142

Fitness, custody test: 75–76, 78

Fletz, Ray: 138

Florida, reform in: 32–33, 185; alimony, 64–65; custody, 78

Foss, Bob: 128

Foster, Henry: 10, 41–42, 52, 53–54, 74–75, 76, 80, 86–87, 95, 102–103

Fox, Arthur: 16

Freed, Doris: 76

Friedan, Betty: 53

"Full Faith and Credit," Constitutional doctrine: custody matters, 94–95; foreign decrees, 164; migratory divorce, 157–158

Gehrels, Kathryn: 25, 61–62

Georgia, alimony: 57

Ginty, Helen: 85

Gitter, Max: 14, 46, 47

Goddard, Wendell: 60, 61

Goldstein, Joseph: 14, 46, 47

Good, Francis: 65

Governor's Commission on the Family (Calif.): 19, 49, 111–112, 145, 150–151

Grad, Corinne: 53

Griswold, Erwin: 143, 149

Gross, Harriet: 128

Grounds, fault theory: cause of marital problems and, 12–13; and custody, 75–76, 77–78, 79–84; elimination proposed, 183–185; establishing, 2, 5, 13; fabricated evidence, 5, 7; mongrelization, 38–39, 43–44

Groups, reformist: 136–139

Grunsky, Donald: 28–29

Haiti, migratory divorce: 166–167

Halperin, Donald: 69–71

Hamilton, Alexander: 142

Hansen, Paul: 136–137, 139

Harrington, Paul: 147–148

Hask, V. L.: 130

Hawke, Lee: 14

Hawkins, Prince: 163–164

Healy, Regina: 141

Henderson, Laurens: 100, 110

Hofstadter, Samuel: 52–53

Hogoboom, William: 177–178

Hostility between spouses: 180; and alimony, 59, 62; custody matters, 76–77

Idaho, reform in: 38; residency period, 157, 161; Sun Valley, 161–162

Illinois, reform in: 152

Incompatibility: 13, 38–39, 47, 162

In re the Marriage of McKim: 23, 26, 132

Insanity, as a ground: 19

Insurance, divorce: 68–71

Iowa, reform in: 32, 185; custody, 80; no-fault standard, 32; premarital counseling, 178–179

Irreconcilable differences, California standard: 19, 121–122; meaning, 21–22

Irremediable breakdown, no-fault standard: 183–184; California, 19, 21

Jale, William: 24

Justice for Divorced and Separated Mothers: 139–140, 142

Kaplan, Kenneth: 165

Katz, Sanford: 48, 88

Kay, Herma: 21, 24, 29–30, 38, 54, 80, 81, 89, 111, 112, 116, 134, 139

Kennedy, Florynce: 53

Kennedy, John F.: 134

Kennedy, Robert F.: 144

Kentucky, reform in: 36

Kiernan, Cornelius: 148

Kinsey, A. C.: 13

Klein, S. William: 50